"I am protected, I am complete, I am joyful and I am hereby proclaiming that I learned all these things reading Cloris Kylie's new book, *Magnificent...Married or Not*. Thank you, Cloris, for shining a flashlight into the dark corners of divorce and showing us that the big, bad boogie monsters are nothing but lovable pussy cats."

—Pam Grout, author of the *New York Times* bestseller,
*E-Squared: Nine Do-It-Yourself Energy Experiments
That Prove Your Thoughts Create Your Reality*

"Cloris Kylie's breakthrough, master guide shows us how to be our best and to live in awareness during and after the breakdown of a marriage. Spiritual, yet practical, the lessons in this book allow for healing but also for turning this challenging situation into an opportunity for positive change and growth."

—Elizabeth Hamilton-Guarino, author of
PERCOLATE - Let Your Best Self Filter Through and
CEO/Founder of The Best Ever You Network

"In *Magnificent... Married or Not*, Cloris Kylie combines the practicality of a survival guide with the compassionate insight of a wise friend. At its core, it is a roadmap to healing and self-awareness. Cloris explores and peels away the unhealthy expectations and unspoken messages we can bring to relationships and bring to bear upon ourselves. By shedding light on the baggage that often accompanies our connections, she helps us view ourselves instead through a prism of self-worth and rich potential. In doing so, Cloris helps us to navigate our challenges with dignity and poise."

—Alicia Young, author of *The Savvy Girl's Guide to Grace:
small touches with big impact - at home, work and in love*

"Cloris Kylie has woven together an incredibly honest, inspiring and practical book with *Magnificent... Married or Not*. This book not only provides a uniquely spiritual approach to dealing with the difficult aspects in the breakdown of a relationship, but also presents the reader with the opportunity to embrace their own divine spiritual development. The thorough combination of practical tools, real life examples and collected wisdom makes this book a must-read for anyone that values not only enlightened relationships but a deeply conscious and fulfilling life."

—Prudence Grace Holling, author of *Grace Has a Secret*

"*Magnificent...Married or Not* is a real treasure! Beautifully written, Cloris Kylie draws on personal experience and inner wisdom to show you how best to handle marital breakdown in enlightened and empowering ways. If you want to move forward, heal your life, love, and set yourself free from the emotional pain of separation and divorce, you must read this awe-inspiring book. It's magnificent!"

—Helen Martino-Bailey, author of *Journey of Our Spirit* and *Abundance of Joy*

"I have never been divorced but my wife did pass away when she was thirty-four. So I know well the sense of helplessness one can feel after not having someone you once loved in your life. What I didn't know at the time, and what this author so brilliantly conveys, are the tools that can be so helpful in the healing journey. I didn't have this wonderful resource, but you do. It is a treasure trove for anyone who is going through, or has experienced, a divorce. It will not only help you get to the other side but come out with a higher sense of your world and yourself."

—Allen Klein, author of *The Healing Power of Humor* and *Learning to Laugh When You Feel Like Crying*

"*Magnificent...Married or Not - Reaching Your Highest Self Before, During and After Divorce* is a passionate book about rediscovering yourself. Although I have not had the experience of divorce and have been married for more than 20 years, I can appreciate the content in this book. I found it interesting and also helpful in realizing my true potential. If you're in a situation where divorce seems likely, I would recommend this book. It will help you pick up the pieces and shed the negativity surrounding this difficult situation."

—Hilary JM Topper, MPA, President/
CEO of HJMT Public Relations Inc.

"Magnificent...Married or Not is a storehouse of practical wisdom. Cloris Kylie's ability to recognize real-life situations is remarkable, as is her ability to identify the gut feelings we experience when something we treasured is taken away from us. She is equally clear in highlighting specific actions and attitudes that either drain our energy, or point us on the path to a happier existence.

Cloris directs the book especially to people who have been 'left behind,' people who have lost something that they did not choose to lose. I believe that the book is also eminently useful for people who may be choosing to leave a relationship – or a job – or a career – that no longer suits their highest self. Not a selfish higher self, but the being who is meant to bring light and life to this world.

Magnificent...Married or Not provides a much-needed handbook for anyone experiencing a loss, whether the loss is ancient or fresh, whether personal or professional. I look forward to referring it to many of my clients. It will indeed give them an oasis in their overwhelm"

—Millie Grenough, author of *OASIS in the Overwhelm:
60-second strategies for balance in a busy world* and Clinical
Instructor in Psychiatry at Yale University School of Medicine

MAGNIFICENT...
Married or Not

*Reaching your Highest Self Before,
During, and After Divorce*

CLORIS KYLIE

BALBOA
PRESS

A DIVISION OF HAY HOUSE

Balboa Press books may be ordered through booksellers or by contacting:

Balboa Press
A Division of Hay House
1663 Liberty Drive
Bloomington, IN 47403
www.balboapress.com
1 (877) 407-4847

Because of the dynamic nature of the Internet, any web addresses or links contained in this book may have changed since publication and may no longer be valid. The views expressed in this work are solely those of the author and do not necessarily reflect the views of the publisher, and the publisher hereby disclaims any responsibility for them.

The author of this book does not dispense medical advice or prescribe the use of any technique as a form of treatment for physical, emotional, or medical problems without the advice of a physician, either directly or indirectly. The intent of the author is only to offer information of a general nature to help you in your quest for emotional and spiritual well-being. In the event you use any of the information in this book for yourself, which is your constitutional right, the author and the publisher assume no responsibility for your actions.

Any people depicted in stock imagery provided by Thinkstock are models, and such images are being used for illustrative purposes only. Certain stock imagery © Thinkstock.

Printed in the United States of America.

ISBN: 978-1-4525-9323-4 (sc)
ISBN: 978-1-4525-9324-1 (hc)
ISBN: 978-1-4525-9325-8 (e)

Library of Congress Control Number: 2014903578

Balboa Press rev. date: 3/27/14

To Mom,
for your unconditional love,

and

to Dr. Wayne W. Dyer,
for reminding me where I come from.

Contents

PART 2: FROM EGO TO YOUR HIGHEST SELF

PART 3: TOOLS FOR THE JOURNEY

PART 4: THE POWER OF YOUR HIGHEST SELF

Preface

Someone I never met in person suggested I write this book. I only know her Internet name, not her real name, but I know she lives in London. And I know that she went through hell with her marriage, just like I did. She was part of my online support group, which I joined when I had run out of ideas about how to save my marriage. This group was one of the pillars that supported me during the greatest challenge I have ever endured, and I also would never have survived my journey of nearly three years had I not established a strong connection with my divine nature, which I deepened and refined as the months went by.

My connection with Spirit wasn't always like it is today.

I grew up Catholic, and spent fourteen of the first seventeen years of my life in an all-girls Catholic school. Going to church was part of my homework. I even had to write a weekly report on the homily from Sunday service. Like everyone else in my community, I saw myself as separate from God. I believed God was a mystical entity up in heaven who kept track of who was good and bad, and demanded constant praise. This God would select a few people to help and others to abandon or punish until they were purged of their sins. God was a fairy tale, like a Santa Claus for adults. God was watching, so if I was "good," my wishes would be granted. If I was naughty, I would go to hell.

In college, my spirituality changed. I found myself going to church because I wanted to, not because my grades depended on it. I found myself yearning for closer contact with God. And that's how

I started talking to Spirit. Spirit replied by providing me with the peace and comfort I sought. However, my connection to God was still immature. Although I would ask for guidance, I would also ask for help with the day-to-day problems of my existence. I'd pray, *God, help me get over this cold quicker. God, make this guy I really like notice me.* Many times, in return for his help, I would offer what I perceived as a sacrifice, such as going for a month without chocolate. But even though my view of God was still egotistical, my yearning for a real connection with Spirit had been unleashed and could no longer be stopped.

I went to graduate school immediately after college, and it was at the university's Catholic retreat where I met my husband. He wasn't a practicing Catholic, but like me was in search of a spiritual identity. During that retreat, I was exposed to meditation as a way to achieve conscious contact with God. After that, I felt an even stronger yearning for a true connection with Spirit, but somehow I wasn't fulfilled by my regular church attendance any longer. I was looking for something different; I just didn't know what it was.

It wasn't until years after completing my graduate degree that I came across Dr. Wayne Dyer's *Inspiration.* The book changed my life. Every word resonated with me in a new and exciting way.

Intuitively, I already knew that God wasn't a "cosmic bellboy," as Dyer calls our flawed image of God in his book. My eyes were opened to the truths that God has unconditional love for everyone, and that God and each of us are one.

Internalizing the reality of my own divine self (my Highest Self) took me years. I had received the information, but only partly digested it. I knew *about* the nature of my connection with the Divine, but I didn't *know it* because I hadn't completely experienced it. My yearning for more drove me to read more of Dr. Dyer's books, as well as the works of inspirational masters such as Eckhart Tolle, Anthony de Mello, and Neville Goddard. This information transformed my view of God and religion. Though I continued to consider myself a Christian, I had gained a different perspective on the world and my role in it.

I thought I had finally created a true connection with Spirit, but it wasn't until my life was being turned upside down, it wasn't until after I had the metaphorical rug of my marriage pulled from under my feet, that I realized I hadn't been tested at all. It wasn't until then that I realized I still had a lot to learn. As I embarked on the journey of recovering from betrayal, abandonment, and the breakdown of my marriage, I was forced to become aware of my shortcomings. My sense of self was threatened because I had become deeply attached to my husband and to my marriage. It was only toward the end of this journey that I realized I had completed an intensive course in spiritual growth. Only at this point was I able really to *see* that I was capable of making a leap from knowing *about* to really *knowing* my divine nature. I *knew* it then because I had experienced it.

With that discovery, everything changed.

I can't say that my spiritual growth is complete even now, but I've certainly learned and grown enough that I feel called to help others—people like you—who are going through a painful experience similar to mine. This book is for those who feel they are alone in their struggle to save their marriage, or those who resisted the end of their marriage and yet were left behind.

Your spouse might have abandoned you emotionally, even if you're living together. Your spouse might have physically moved out to "figure things out." Your spouse might have filed for divorce. You might have recently signed your divorce papers. You might have been divorced years ago, but your emotions are as raw as though it just happened. If those things have happened, then this book is for you.

If you're holding this book in your hands, then I know you're already listening to the inner guidance of Spirit. My intent is that you will be able to see yourself reflected in my experience, and avoid the pain you would have suffered had you not connected to your divine nature. I want to bring you to a state of peace sooner rather than later. Even if you cannot or could not save your marriage, I want you to save yourself.

I also want you to see the possibilities that lie ahead for you. I want you to tap into the divine power within you. I want you to realize that once you recognize your connection to this power, all things are possible. These hopes are my motivation to share my story and lessons with you.

I love you.

Introduction

*"When we are no longer able to change a situation
we are challenged to change ourselves."*
—Viktor Frankl

The subtitle of *Magnificent... Married or Not* is *Reaching Your Highest Self Before, During, and After Divorce.* Your first question might be, "Exactly what is my Highest Self?"

Your Highest Self is the omnipotent, omnipresent, almighty force that created everything in the universe, including you. Connecting with your Highest Self does not only mean to become aware that you're a divine creation, but to *know* that the Divine is within you, and therefore, *is* you. I was introduced to the concept of the Highest Self through *Wishes Fulfilled*, by Wayne Dyer. In this book, Dyer explains how "you move from being a spark or a fragment of God to being able to assert that *I am God* and not feel as if you are committing blasphemy or a cardinal sin by such a declaration." [1]

When you connect to your Highest Self, miracles start to happen because you can directly tap into the power of the divine within you, and I want you to be able to tap into this power because it's then when you'll truly be able to live a life of meaning.

Why connect with your Highest Self now? Because big life challenges, such as separation and divorce, are usually catalysts of big personal changes. As Nikos Kazantzakis says in *Saint Francis*, "The further down you gain your momentum, the higher you shall be able to reach." [2] Your situation may have caused you to sink so low emotionally that you are now in position to propel yourself up to the highest and purest energy: the energy of God.

Magnificent... Married or Not is intended to be your companion. My hope is that you'll feel supported and encouraged by my book to clean your connection with the Divine within you. You'll know there's hope for you. Now.

Magnificent... Married or Not is organized into four basic parts. Part One will introduce you to the fields of energy inside and around you. You'll see yourself reflected in the negative energy emotions that are likely to surface during and after separation or divorce, and you'll realize you are not alone. Then, you'll learn strategies to nullify the negative energies in your life so you are free to be happy. You will also understand how the Law of Attraction works in your situation, and how to use it to turn your life around.

Part Two will help you see if and how your ego is preventing you from reaching your Highest Self. Your ego is the part of you that believes you are your material possessions, your job, your relationships, and your reputation. You'll replace disconnection with connection, attachment with detachment, resistance with allowing, and blame with taking ownership of your current situation.

Part Three will provide you with the following powerful tools for your healing journey.

- *Your Imagination.* You'll explore the power of your conscious thoughts to reprogram your subconscious mind, and the power of assuming the feeling of your wish fulfilled to manifest healing and happiness.
- *The Way to Learn.* You'll understand the three main ways to attract lessons in life, and identify which of these methods leads to the minimal amount of pain.
- *The Role of an Open Mind.* You'll see how keeping a mind open to all possibilities during the seemingly uncertain future will help you take advantage of present and future opportunities.

- *Patience.* As you embark on this "thousand-mile journey," you'll realize the importance of *knowing* that everything you desire will be delivered to you in divine order.
- *Meditation.* You'll learn to demystify meditation so you can most effectively incorporate this practice into your daily life.

Once you have learned how to nullify negative energy emotions, tame the ego, and adopt the tools explained in Part Three, you'll be ready to tap into the power of your Highest Self, which is explored in Part Four. You'll not only be healed, but will experience true miracles. The right people and events will show up into your life at exactly the right time.

By connecting with your Highest Self, you'll honor your magnificence and experience synchronicity, and everything will be possible for you.

I encourage you to review Appendix A of this book, which includes techniques to handle special situations, such as selecting and working with attorneys, conducting peaceful divorce negotiations, questioning whether you should remarry your ex-spouse, overcoming negative emotions evoked by milestones like the final date of your divorce, and being faced with your spouse's new romantic relationships. Lastly, Appendix B includes a list of topics for reflection that will help you clarify your thoughts and receive intuitive messages to guide you in the future.

Take all the time you need to read this book and to really *see* the truths in it. Be patient and kind to yourself. Be forgiving if you slide back into old patterns. All human beings do so—though some more often than others. Regardless of how often you slip, and how many times, you'll be aware of your divine nature—and this extraordinary awareness will put you back on track to experiencing a magnificent life.

God bless you.

Author's Note

Through this book, I'll use the terms "God," and "Spirit" interchangeably. These names represent the divine presence that lives inside of you and is embedded in every element of creation. The subconscious mind represents the mind of the Divine.

I'll call my ex-husband my "husband" throughout the book, because I will be referring to the experience I had when I was still married to him.

Similarly, I'll call the person who has left you your "spouse," even though your divorce might have already been finalized.

There's no specific time in the continuum of abandonment designated to experience the spiritual shift that will allow you to connect with your Highest Self. Whether you just separated from your spouse or have been divorced for years, the time for spiritual growth is *now*.

PART ONE

Energy

CHAPTER 1

Your Place in the Energy Spectrum

"If you want to find the secrets of the universe, think in terms of energy, frequency, and vibration."
—Nikola Tesla

The universe is a bundle of energy. There is energy that you can see, touch, and smell in the tangible world, such as the energy of a peanut butter sandwich, and there is also energy you can subconsciously feel in the intangible world, such as the energy of the electromagnetic field around your cellphone. Low- or slow-energy frequencies are associated with the tangible world, while fast- or high-energy frequencies are associated with that which is invisible to the human eye.

Several scholars have explored the concept of energy fields and their relationship to our states of being. I find that Wayne Dyer's interpretation is one of the easiest to understand. In *There's a Spiritual Solution to Every Problem*, Dyer asserts that:[1]

1.   *Everything vibrates, everything moves.*
2.   *Faster vibrations mean getting closer to "spirit."*
3.   *Slower vibrations keep us in the world of "problems."*
4.   *You can choose to eliminate whatever interferes with increasing your vibrational field.*

1

5. *You can negotiate the presence of factors in your life to increase your frequency of vibrations.*

Emotions such as anger, fear, and shame are rooted in low-energy fields. Joy, forgiveness, and compassion belong to high-energy fields. The energy field with the highest vibration is that of God (love). The energy of Spirit is intangible, but we can subconsciously feel the presence of this omnipotent force in our lives.

I suggest you close your eyes and ask yourself if you have ever felt that there is an omnipotent, omnipresent, immutable form of energy that allowed you to grow and develop from a cluster of cells in your mother's womb to a human being. I'm certain your answer will be yes. You know deep in your heart that this energy is the same that guides a flock of migrating geese or starts the blossoming of trees in the spring. This is the energy that drives you to love others. This energy has led you to read this book.

What is the role of energy during the breakdown of your marriage? Chances are you have aligned yourself with low-energy fields, which are dragging you away from Spirit. You want to heal and be truly happy, but this can only occur when you have cleaned your connection with your Highest Self by rising to higher energy fields.

Note that I say you need to "clean your connection" rather than to "establish connection." The reason is that regardless of what you have done or felt in the past, or the way you feel now, the connection already exists.

Let's draw an analogy between the connection with your Highest Self and a phone connection. If the phone line isn't working properly, you won't be able to understand what the other person is saying, you'll miss portions of the conversation, or you might not even be able to contact the other person. If the connection is clean and strong, you'll be able to fully communicate and enjoy the conversation. The connection was there all along; it only needed to be freed of interference.

When your connection with your Highest Self is clean, you move toward God realization. When you are God realized, your spiritual connection is so pure that there's no pain or suffering in your life. When you are God realized, problems disappear.

Achieving complete God realization might not be possible for you. After all, there have only been a few human beings on this planet who have thoroughly and immutably cleaned their connection with their own divinity. But by moving toward a higher energy field, you will *know* you are on the right path. You'll experience the happiness that results from being on this path.

David Hawkins, M.D., Ph.D., completed one of the most compelling studies about human consciousness. In his book, *Power vs. Force*, Dr. Hawkins explains the result of twenty years of investigation to calibrate the energy of people, objects, and feelings. Hawkins used the outcome of his kinesiology tests to create a map of consciousness, which uses a logarithmic scale from zero (death) to 1,000 (pure divinity).[2] The slowest energies are clustered in the lower range of the scale, with shame calibrating 20 on the scale, dangerously close to death. Levels below 200 are destructive, and represent "force." Levels above 200 are constructive, and represent "power." In short, the 200 level is the threshold at which humans start to be aligned with Spirit. Since most people calibrate below 200 even if they aren't feeling distressed, people in your situation will usually sink below the 200 level for extended periods of time—sometimes for the rest of their lives.

Per Hawkins, clinical kinesiology muscle testing shows that negative mental stimuli (low-energy fields) produce physical weakness. Learning how kinesiology works allowed me to understand why my anger and sadness had made me ill. My hair was falling out, my skin was breaking out, and a general feeling of malaise was part of my day-to-day existence.

Being aware of the existence of high-energy and low-energy fields will allow you to understand the physical manifestations of your current thoughts and emotions. The most common symptoms of depression are sleep disturbances, a sense of sadness, irritability, a change in appetite, restlessness, fatigue, feelings of worthlessness, trouble thinking, crying spells, back pain, headaches, and loss of interest in daily activities. As you can see, symptoms of depression are nothing more than symptoms of your alignment with low-energy fields. Slow-energy frequencies result in physical weakness. Fast-energy frequencies result in physical strength.

Being aware of where you are in the energy spectrum is the first step into moving toward faster energies and, as a result, toward becoming your strongest and Highest Self.

CHAPTER 2

Sinking into Low-Energy Fields

*"The angry, condemning person who sends out
destructive thoughts, feeling, or speech to another who
is poised in his own God power, receives back to himself
the quality with which he charged this power."*
—Master Saint Germain

Regardless of your country of origin, culture, and socioeconomic status, you'll experience feelings similar to those of other people who have gone through, or are going through, separation and divorce, because you and they share the same fountain of human consciousness. You're connected to every person on the planet, so it's likely that you'll see your own feelings reflected on the list below, which is based on my memories.

No matter what your negative feelings are or how much they have weakened you emotionally and physically, I want you to take comfort in knowing you're not alone.

The low-energy feelings I experienced were:

- *Petrification:* Paralyzing fear
- *Emptiness:* An internal void
- *Hopelessness:* No vision of a happy future
- *Worthlessness:* A negative perception of self
- *Defeat:* A sense of failure

- *Anger:* A state of frustration
- *Thirst for justice:* "Not fair" thinking
- *Guilt:* Self-blame
- *Regret:* Looking back at past decisions
- *Uncertainty:* Perception of an unsafe future
- *Loneliness:* No "special" connection

Let's explore each one of these feelings and how they might impact your life.

Petrification: Paralyzing Fear

I'm not talking about usual fears. I'm talking about *paralyzing* fear, the kind that makes you want to hide under a rock. This fear makes the world around you seem unwelcoming and just plain dangerous. Even if you consider yourself a model of self-assurance and strength, you can still become paralyzed when your marriage breaks down.

I remember driving to board the train to New York City. I had completed this trip many times without trouble, but this particular trip took place shortly after my husband filed for divorce. I was afraid to drive to the station, but still hopped in the car. While on the highway, I fought the insistent urge to turn around and imagined my car careening out of control. Once I arrived at the station, I waited to buy the ticket until I realized I would miss the train if I didn't take immediate action. Ticket in hand, while waiting for the train, I considered going back home. I was petrified. Everyone around me seemed indifferent or hostile. Danger seemed to be lurking on the train tracks, behind the pillars, under the stairs.

I also felt fearful at night. My fear was stirred by nothing in particular, but I still had to double-check that the doors were locked. My dreams often turned into nightmares in which I was being chased or was in high danger. Once awake, I would picture a life away from my husband, and a sharp pang of fear would hit my stomach.

Fear became nearly a constant in my life. And ironically, every time my husband behaved in ways that hinted he might want to return to our marriage, I also experienced fear. I wondered whether I'd be betrayed once more, and whether I'd be able to withstand the pain of that experience again.

I didn't know what to do, or what to make of my terror. I had always been a very intuitive person, but my gut feeling and intuition were silenced. I wasn't sure if the voice inside that told me I was at risk was the voice of God or the voice of fear.

Emptiness: An Internal Void

The breakdown of your marriage probably left a huge void inside of you, as though someone physically sucked a huge chunk of matter out of your gut. In my case, the feeling was intense every time my husband mentioned "moving on" or "going our separate ways." The feeling lingered for longer periods after he made it official that he was leaving me and our marriage. Even immediately after a meal, I felt as though I hadn't had anything to eat in days.

When you're feeling empty, it seems that the only person who can "fix" this emptiness is your spouse. Friends, family, or even your children cannot fill the void. And when well-intentioned people say, "You're a great person! You will find someone else!" you could feel even emptier.

Hopelessness: No Vision of a Happy Future

When you sink down to low-energy fields, you might start to believe that your destiny is to exist in this unhappiness forever. If you're still unsure of the future of your marriage, you might lose hope to be able to save it and picture yourself signing divorce papers. You might also lose hope in your ability to function without your spouse.

If you have already gone through the divorce, you might lose hope of finding a new partner.

When my husband filed for divorce, my despair was so strong that it immobilized me. My legs felt heavier when I walked. I was so distracted that I often would misplace things, miss appointments, and leave doors unlocked. Because I was investing all my energy in my sadness, I was living my life on autopilot.

Hopelessness and sadness grow when you fuel them with thoughts about what happened, what could have been, and what you could have done differently. If you tried to save your marriage for an extended period of time and realized that your efforts were not going to pan out, hopelessness was probably the first emotion to hit.

While I was trying to save my marriage, I would combat my sense of hopelessness with supposed hope. I hoped to turn things around and renew my relationship with my husband. It all made sense in my mind. When he called, hope would return. When he didn't call, hopelessness would take over. As an outsider, you may see how my emotional state depended on my husband's behavior. I was a prisoner of my own attachment. You may also see how I remained in a state of hoping, which is a state of lack. Finally, you may see how I assumed that if I worked really hard to save my marriage, I would achieve my goal.

I didn't realize that working hard to achieve something is not a guarantee of success. Working hard to achieve something and visualizing yourself succeeding are very powerful tools, but their power will depend on whether your desires are aligned with your Highest Self. We'll explore the power of visualization in Part Three of this book.

Worthlessness: A Negative Perception of Self

Being left behind in your marriage, whether or not it was for another person, is one of the strongest forms of rejection you'll experience. You're being rejected by the person you called your soul mate, life partner, and family. Such rejection might make you feel unworthy of love. You might compare yourself to others and conclude that everyone who's in a romantic relationship must be better than you. Otherwise, why were you abandoned and not them?

My experiences with separation and divorce strongly impacted my sense of self-worth. My husband's rationalization to justify his infidelity and his decision to leave me was that I had too many flaws. I thought that something was wrong with me if I couldn't meet all of his expectations. I thought that I hadn't worked hard enough to be like everyone else, or at least to be as perfect as my husband wanted me to be.

Feeling worthless has myriad negative ramifications in your life, and I consider it to be one of the most dangerous negative emotions you might experience. If you are worthless, you are not lovable. If you feel unlovable, you'll avoid others so no one can judge you, you'll treat your body poorly, and you'll be incapable of extending love to those around you.

Defeat: A Sense of Failure

When your spouse told you he or she was considering divorce, you probably did whatever you thought you could to rescue your marriage.

You probably:

- Bought marriage-saving books and tried to engage your spouse in your efforts to rescue the relationship.
- Pleaded for him or her to reconsider.
- Tried to prove why your spouse's decision was a mistake.
- Became needy and clingy.
- Bargained to make your spouse stay.

In short, you put all your energy into what wasn't working in your life: your marriage.

This is exactly what I did. Despite my efforts, my journey of nearly three years spent investing all my energy in my failing marriage still resulted in divorce. You might be wondering why I continued my efforts for such a long time. The reason is that I grew up believing that if I did my best to achieve a goal, I would achieve it. I was shocked that the outcome of my hard work wasn't what I had expected. One of my core beliefs had been shattered. I felt defeated, and you might feel as though you've lost a battle, too.

Anger: A State of Frustration

You might be really angry. Enraged, in fact. With hopelessness and failure usually comes frustration, and with frustration, usually comes anger. The anger might come and go, or it could settle into a dark corner inside you to fester for a long time.

Anger will make you impatient and short tempered. Anger will make you snap at your loved ones. Anger will steal your sleep and make your heart race in the darkness of the night. Anger will cloud your thinking. Anger will take over your life if you let it.

Anger was one of the most debilitating feelings I experienced. I was physically weakened by my anger, and couldn't concentrate on anything else but my negative emotions. Instead of dissipating, my angry thoughts usually led to more insistent anger, because I was neurotically angry about being so angry. I had a sense of separation from love. I felt hatred. I wanted to break something. I wanted to hit someone. I didn't like people. I was short tempered, impatient. And when I thought I had finally overcome anger, it would come back, usually after something triggered a bad memory or after my husband said or did something that I would find hurtful or offensive.

Thirst for Justice: "Not Fair" Thinking

"This is not fair!" you probably say to yourself. Your friends and relatives tell you that you don't deserve to be rejected in such a way by the person who promised to be by your side for the rest of your life.

The sense of there being unfairness in your life leads to frustration, and as you already know, frustration leads to anger. You're not a horrible person, so why is this horrible thing happening to you? Bad things should not happen to good people, right? Good things are not supposed to happen to bad people such as your spouse, who is apparently having an amazing time on his or her own. The thirst for "justice" kicks in. You want to "get even." As a result, you fall into the trap of revenge, which we'll explore in the next chapter of this book.

Guilt: Self-Blame

As your marriage falls apart, you'll list all the possible actions you took to drive your partner away. You might use up most of your waking hours to analyze each memory of your interactions with your spouse. As beneficial as this may be for you to determine your role in the breakdown of your marriage, you'll accumulate a fair amount of guilt.

I felt into the guilt trap. I regretted things I did and said, and some of those things were as insignificant as not watching my husband's favorite TV show with him. I desperately wanted to turn back time. I apologized for what I had done wrong, and actively worked on eliminating the behavioral patterns I thought I needed to change. Nonetheless, the outcome of my situation remained the same. My "failure" to save my marriage stirred additional guilt-producing thoughts in me.

If you feel guilty, you'll subconsciously want your spouse to feel guilty, too. You can only give away what you have inside, which in this case is guilt. You might assume the role of a victim, and tell your spouse how much he or she is hurting you. Although you might be successful in instilling feelings of guilt in your spouse, adding this negative emotion to an already negative mix is likely to worsen your situation. Your spouse will associate seeing you with feeling guilty, and will put even more distance between the two of you.

Guilt is at the bottom of Hawkins' map of human consciousness, which I described earlier. By feeling and instilling guilt, you bring yourself and your relationship to low-energy, weakening fields.

Regret: Looking Back at Past Decisions

Guilt and regret usually go hand in hand. Your guilt might produce regret about your behavior during your marriage, the separation, or the divorce proceedings. Just as I did, you might regret the years you "wasted" trying to save your marriage. You might even regret meeting your spouse and marrying in the first place.

Regret is using your present moments to wish your past was different, which is impossible. Because regret leads to a dead-end road, sorrow and frustration are the usual results.

Regret is also accompanied by shame, which along with guilt ranks the lowest in the map of human consciousness. If you're regretful, you'll be physically weakening yourself.

Uncertainty: Perception of an Unsafe Future

You thought you could count on your spouse to be with you for the rest of your life. You had plans for the future. You revealed your inner self to your spouse, as you never revealed it to anyone before. Then, when you were at your most vulnerable, your spouse yanked your security blanket away from you.

Psychologist Abraham Maslow developed a Hierarchy of Human Needs to explain people's motivation and behavior, which has been represented as a pyramid with five different levels. From bottom to top, such needs can be categorized as physiological needs for survival, safety needs, love and connection, self-esteem, and self-actualization. As you can see, safety and security are one of the most basic human needs, placed second from the bottom on Maslow's pyramid. When you consider yourself abandoned, life won't feel safe anymore, so your inclination will be to focus on how to eliminate your perceived lack of safety. Your family is changing, your place of residence and career might be changing, and your routines are changing. You'll want to find something stable on which you can rely. The need for stability might drive you to desperately cling to what's left of your marriage even if the divorce has already been filed or to decide to stay in your house "for the children" even if you know you cannot financially afford it on your own. Even if you put aside the added pain that these decisions may bring into your life, striving to regain safety will place you in a position of non-safety and rob you of the precious present moment.

Loneliness: No "Special" Connection

One of the most common comments from people who have been left by their spouses is that they miss that special someone with whom they could share their day-to-day existence. They miss the connection. They feel as though there's no one to turn to if "something bad" happens. If their children are living with them, they may not be physically alone, but they can still feel lonely.

Even if you were comfortable being alone in the past, your recent loss might make being in your own company intolerable. Mornings and nights might be the loneliest times for you, as they were for me. You might find yourself turning on the TV just to hear voices around you. You might feel alienated when you are in a large crowd. When loneliness becomes your companion, other low-energy feelings, such as sadness, anger, and fear, usually join in.

Ready to move on to an uplifting topic? Continue to the next chapter.

CHAPTER 3

Rising to High-Energy Fields

"Choose only the good and the great and
the beautiful. The rest is delusion."
—Uell S. Andersen

Running low probably left you exhausted.

Now you're ready for answers, aren't you?

Not necessarily. In fact, you're ready only if you choose to be ready. You have the power to elevate your consciousness, but you'll only be able to use this power when you make an internal decision to do so.

Choosing High Energy

If you choose to continue functioning in a low-energy field, you'll be aligning yourself with unhappiness. Your physical body will be so weakened by your sustained association with slower and lower energies that illness will have a chance to take over. You'll become a bitter person who attracts circumstances that lead to more bitterness.

Later in this book, we'll talk about the Law of Attraction applied to a person going through separation or divorce, so you'll be able to see how the universe reacts to your negative feelings by providing you with more experiences that match the low-energy field you are in.

You picked up this book because you intuitively knew that you needed to raise your level of consciousness. Your Highest Self is pure joy, and it's asking you to return to the state of joy that is innately yours. The first step in the journey toward joy is *awareness*.

Awareness

Awareness is such an important and pervasive element for a clean connection with your Highest Self that we'll explore it in several sections of this book. Let's start by illustrating the concept of awareness with a simple example that you've no doubt seen many times.

Picture a dog that has a problem with bicycles. The dog is perfectly content walking alongside its owner. Then, a cyclist approaches. The dog's reaction is not immediate. It takes a few seconds for the image of the bicycle to translate into thoughts of fear, which then take physical form in a frenzy of barking and growling. Dog trainers get rid of this behavior by distracting the dog with a treat *before* it's overtaken by a negative emotion. The trainers know that once the emotion has taken over, even the juiciest piece of steak won't stop the dog's aggressive behavior.

You can raise your level of consciousness by being aware of thoughts that lead to low-energy emotions, and immediately selecting a new thought to think. Note that I'm not suggesting that you *resist* the initial thought or *fight* the thought. Later on, you'll learn that resisting and fighting will only strengthen the thought. What I suggest is that, by exercising awareness, you become an observer to your own negative thoughts. Acting as an observer will allow you to enter a place of complete calm and to replace damaging thoughts with thoughts that are aligned with high-energy emotions. As James Thurber said, "Let us not look back in anger, nor forward in fear, but around in awareness."[1]

"I Am..." Affirmations

The second step in your journey from low-energy fields to high-energy fields is to reframe what you consider to be true about yourself.

The phrase "I am" has been the focus of attention for several spiritual masters, including Neville Goddard in *The Power of Awareness,* the ascended master Saint Germain in *The "I Am" Discourses,* Sri Nisargadatta Maharaj (one of the great Indian sages) in *I Am That,* and more recently, James Twyman in *The Moses Code* and Wayne W. Dyer in *Wishes Fulfilled.* According to the Old Testament, "I am" is the name God used to identify himself when Moses encountered the burning bush. By saying, "I am...," you're calling upon divine power.

For me, the words *I am* would have no power unless they were said with a specific intention (either positive or negative). I believe that the power of "I am" resides in our self-identification within it. By saying, "I am...," you're defining who you are, your true essence, your Self. So if you say, "I am sad," "I am angry," or "I am lonely," you're identifying your true essence with sadness, anger, and loneliness. In order to be joyful, you must change the concept of yourself from victim to qualities that are aligned with Spirit (the place where you originated).

As you move toward joy, I encourage you to replace your old negative statements of self-identification with statements that reflect your divine nature.

Replace. . .	With. . .
I am petrified	I am protected
I am empty inside	I am complete
I am hopeless	I am joyful
I am worthless	I am love
I am defeated	I am learning and growing
I am angry	I am forgiving
I am demanding justice	I am giving
I am guilty	I am renewed
I am regretful	I am now
I am uncertain	I am safe
I am lonely	I am with my Senior Partner

Let's explore each one of these new affirmations in detail.

"I Am Protected"

If you are protected, fear will be impossible to manifest. I suggest a simple five-step approach to nullify the paralyzing fear that you may be experiencing.

Step 1: Become an observer. Step away from the situation and see yourself from a distance as objectively as you can. What do you see? What do you look like when you're afraid? What are you doing or not doing?

Step 2: Self-check. Use the answers you received in step one to determine how your deep sense of fear is preventing you from living a full life. Have you stopped doing what once brought you joy? Have you been reluctant to try new activities? Have you stopped spending quality time with friends and relatives?

Step 3: Search for the power within. Meditate on the truth that you're a divine creation. Repeat the affirmation, "I am protected," as you visualize your fear being swept away by the power of your Highest Self. Affirm that there's a spark of God inside you, and you can tap into the power of this spark any time you wish to.

Step 4: Reach out. Connect with others, as this is a way to strengthen your connection with your own divine power. This connection might be as subtle as smiling at strangers as you walk past them or complimenting the cashier at the grocery store on her funky necklace. Connection might be calling a relative or friend and telling them how much they mean to you. Connection might be hugging your children more. Only you know which behaviors create a sense of connection for you; list those behaviors, and act upon them.

Step 5: Extend love. Fear cannot exist in the presence of love. Love protects you. If you love yourself and extend that love toward others (including your spouse) your fear will dissolve. We'll talk about love in more depth later in this book.

⚜ ⚜ ⚜

Let's use my story about feeling petrified while waiting for the train to New York City to illustrate a practical application of this five-step approach.

Step 1: I became an observer. I pictured myself disentangling from my body and hovering over the people waiting for the train. I saw myself as a woman leaning against a column. There was no discernible sign of fear, except for the tight expression on my face. I consciously made my face relax.

Step 2: I recognized that I was seriously considering cancelling this trip, which promised to be fun and exciting, in response to my fear.

Step 3: I took a deep breath and closed my eyes. Then, I pictured myself stuffing my fear inside a white box, sealing the box with duct tape, and placing it on a cloud that slowly drifted out of sight. I said to myself, "I am protected. I have nothing to fear. The people around me have their own problems but they're still here, living their lives. I can be as brave as they are."

Step 4: I used my phone to access my online support group, texting to the members, "I'm petrified." A few seconds later, someone wrote that I had perfectly described what she also was feeling, and that she was relieved not to be the only one experiencing fear. By connecting with my online friends, I remembered that I was connected to everyone around me, including the rest of the bystanders at the train station.

Step 5: I loved myself by remembering how resilient I had been throughout my journey of emotional turmoil, and how much I had learned in the process. I expressed my love for others by typing additional words of reassurance to my online friend, and also by smiling at the person standing next to me at the train station, who smiled at me in return. My online friend replied with a warm message of gratitude.

My paralyzing fear dissolved, and I had an amazing time in New York City.

"I Am Complete"

The void you feel in your gut is a physical manifestation of your thoughts of loss. The person that meant the most to you has left your life, taking a part of you with him or her, or so it seems to you now.

You have the power to nullify your feelings of emptiness. I encourage you to try the following strategies to regain your sense of completeness.

Vocalization. Imagine your spouse is in the room, and tell him or her how you feel. He or she won't be there to hear you, but the act of vocalizing will help you better understand yourself and organize the jumble of ideas in your mind.

Even though my husband had already moved out, I would picture him in front of me and would tell him about my feelings. Even though he wasn't physically present, I released the negative emotions inside and experienced relief.

Cultivate awareness of your true nature. Realize that you're a complete and divine being with or without your partner. Well before you met your spouse, when you were very young, it's likely that you didn't question your completeness. As a child, you probably understood you were whole. You're still that same person. The only difference is that whomever you used to share your life with has left, just like your high school classmates left home after graduation, or like a coworker who moved on to another job, or like your children who already left for college. You might say, "But my classmates, coworker, and children are still a part of my life. They didn't dump me!" And I will tell you the difference is in your perception, because if you look at these situations objectively, they all involve a change in the physical distance between you and another person. The same way you don't need your classmates, your coworkers, or your children by your side to survive, you don't need your spouse by your side to survive. The proof is that you are here, reading this book. You're surviving just fine.

My change in perception took place when I connected with people who had known me before I got married, and when I met people who didn't know me when I was married. To them, I was who I was with or without my husband. I drew from their perception of me to strengthen my own perception of completeness.

Understand that relationships are creations of the mind. There's nothing tangible about a relationship. A relationship is a series of thoughts put together by you about the interactions between you and the other person. Following this logic will help you see why someone may have a different concept of his or her relationship with you than your own perception of the relationship, even when the hard facts are the same.

Meditating on this reality was extremely helpful for me. I tried to imagine my relationship with my husband as loving and positive, and this usually materialized into more positive interactions with him, even during our financial negotiations. I was also able to empathize with my husband, who had a different perception of his relationship with me during the year prior to his filing for divorce. Instead of wanting to "correct" him and be right, I chose to see his perception for what it was: his personal interpretation of reality.

Allow instead of fighting. Let the void inside you be what it is, and fill it with thoughts of completeness because you're a complete and magnificent creation. Say out loud, "I am complete," and then turn your attention to the activities and people that bring joy and meaning into your life. Your feelings of emptiness will lessen or even completely dissolve depending on where you are in the healing process.

In my case, feeling complete didn't happen overnight. I experienced several setbacks along the way, which usually took place when I was resisting the feeling of emptiness inside of me. Nullify your feelings of emptiness with love. Be kind and forgiving to yourself as you journey through the healing process.

"I Am Joyful"

To nullify hopelessness, I needed to understand that my emotional attachment to my husband's behavior was producing my unhappiness. Opening my eyes to this truth wasn't easy. I had resisted the idea of divorce for as long as I could, until the pain of rejection forced me to accept that I wasn't going to achieve what I then desired. Even when I reached that place of acceptance, I was still attached to my past, and continued riding waves of sorrow and hopelessness.

I'm not suggesting that you block or bottle up your sadness. Allowing your feelings to arise is the quickest way to eliminate them, because negative (dark) energies will dissipate in the presence of truth (light). However, I urge you to consider that if you give in to the pain for extended periods of time, you'll be wasting the most precious gift you were given: your own life.

I suggest that you meditate on the following three truths:

Truth 1: The attachment trap. Breaking the bonds of emotional attachment is necessary to achieve true happiness. If your happiness depends on your marital status or on your spouse's behavior, you're not truly free. You need to make a conscious choice to be free. In Part Two of this book, we will study attachment in depth as one of the main components of the ego.

Truth 2: Unexpected blessings. Your efforts might not have produced the change you were expecting, but consider other positive results you might have achieved. As Henry David Thoreau said, "All misfortune is but a stepping stone to fortune."[2] Ask yourself what would *not* have happened if your spouse hadn't left. What new friends wouldn't have entered your life? What enriching experiences would you have missed? What would you not know about yourself?

In my case, I achieved what was even more beneficial to my self-actualization than saving my marriage: I became a better person than I used to be, I eliminated the toxic elements of my relationship with my husband, I was able to touch other people's lives by sharing my story and lessons, and I learned to love myself at all times. Regardless of the outcome, I was at peace because I knew I had given my all for the sake of love.

Truth 3: Present choices. You made choices in the past (consciously or subconsciously) that produced a result: your present situation. Independently of what happened in the past, or what might happen in the future, the current reality is that your spouse is gone. And now you are the designer of your new present moments.

In Ernest Hemingway's *Islands in the Stream*, the son of Thomas Hudson, the main character, is killed in battle. Hudson is found dancing at a party the same night his son dies. When someone asks him how he can possibly be out dancing, he replies that he had to get over what happened sooner or later or it would take him, and he

23

chose sooner. This is an extreme example, and I'm not suggesting you emulate Hemingway's character and throw a party if you don't feel it in your heart. However, I do ask you to remember that getting over your pain will eventually have to happen, and it's your choice to decide *when* it happens.

At the beginning and end of your meditation, affirm, "I am joyful." Reinforce your affirmation by aligning yourself with joyful experiences. What gives you joy? Petting a dog? Playing with children? Helping others? Write down all the sources of joy and meaning in your life, and seek to draw upon those sources *now*.

"I Am Love"

To *be* love, you must extend love to yourself, to your spouse, and to everyone and everything on the planet. Withholding love from those who hurt you will prevent you from advancing on the path to your Highest Self.

Loving yourself. If love could be represented as a pyramid, self-love would be at its base. Feeling worthless is a lack of self-love, and if you cannot love yourself, you won't be able to love others. Also, a lack of self-love will prevent you from fully connecting with your Highest Self because by its own nature, love is God and God is love.

How to regain self-love?

First, realize that how much you love yourself is completely independent from your spouse's words and behavior. Self-love comes from inside of you.

Second, spend time on yourself. The changes and additional responsibilities in your life might make it seem as though there is no opportunity for me-time, but you must schedule activities that give you pleasure. Block an hour to exercise or to read a book. Go for a walk in nature. Take a class on a subject you always wanted to study.

Third, take care of yourself. This is very much related to spending time on yourself; and it also has a broader scope. Taking care of yourself means:

- Saying no to events that you don't feel called to attend.
- Feeding your body healthy food.
- Exercising.
- Staying away from habits that weaken you, such as smoking and drinking alcohol.
- Asking for help, especially if you aren't equally sharing the care of your children with your spouse.
- Choosing to see beauty instead of flaws when you look in the mirror.
- Being patient with yourself if you return to harboring negative emotions.
- Meditating.

Fourth, affirm, "I am love" upon awakening and before going to sleep. Feel in your body what *being* love feels like, and contemplate that you're already connected to love because you're connected to God.

Loving your spouse. You can only give away that which you are or what you have, so once you love yourself, you'll be able to extend love to others, including your spouse.

Have you considered that your spouse might feel worthless, too? Have you thought of your spouse as someone who's hurting? Someone who's lost, perhaps? Most people who leave their marriages have done so not only because they feel disconnected from their partners, but also because they're disconnected from their true Selves. Your spouse did only what he or she knew to do with the information he or she had in the circumstances of the moment. Your spouse is not the enemy. You two are and will always be connected, regardless of the physical location where you reside. However, you cannot force or expect your spouse to acknowledge this connection. All you can do is extend love.

By extending love to your spouse, you might help your spouse self-love so he or she is in position to connect with others and to love others again. Keep in mind that the purpose of helping your spouse is not to reconcile, but to simply help him or her. You're giving something of yourself because you're being guided by your Highest Self, and all your Highest Self can do is give.

Loving everyone and everything on the planet. This love includes people whose actions hurt your marriage. "Easier said than done," you might retort, especially if your spouse had an affair or left you for someone else. I can absolutely relate.

No matter how hard or easy, learning to be love is an essential step for you.

Getting to the point where you extend love to all humans might take some time, so be patient with yourself. You don't need to force the loving feelings. I suggest you start by placating your feelings of hatred toward your so-called enemies through adopting emotional neutrality. Once you are in a neutral place within, you'll be ready to raise yourself to a position of love.

Note that loving others doesn't mean to accept or condone their hurtful behavior. Loving those who hurt you means that you view them as part of God's creation, and as people who are acting out of ignorance and disconnection from Spirit rather than out of malice.

Fuel your love for those around you by reveling in the miracles of nature. Take a walk outside and see your surroundings with the eyes of a child. As Rumi, a Persian poet, wrote, "We must become ignorant of what we have been taught and be instead bewildered."[3] Regaining your sense of wonder will allow you to remember your divine origins.

Also, practice appreciation. Cherish a smile from a stranger, or a kind gesture from a relative or a friend. In your mind, these people might be "less important" to you than your spouse, but they're as spiritually connected to you as he or she.

Finally, remember two important truths:

Truth 1: Love is abundant and ready for you to tap into its source, which is God. You are already connected to love. If you feel worthless and incapable of finding love again, think again. Open your heart to receiving love; only then you'll find the love you're yearning for.

Truth 2: To love and to receive love, you must keep an open mind. Depending on where you are in the self-actualization process, love might not reenter your life through a romantic partner. Love might come to you from your children, your parents, friends, or even a stranger who offers you support without being asked. Romantic love will only materialize in your life when you're ready to receive it.

Be love and love will be in your life.

"I Am Learning and Growing"

In Chapter 11 of this book, you'll explore the ways to learn when going through a life challenge such as separation or divorce. For now, I invite you to focus on reframing your current situation by not seeing it as a failure, but as an opportunity to grow. Instead of focusing on what you don't want (defeat) focus on what you do want (a learning experience).

Every time thoughts of defeat pop into your head, affirm, "I am learning. I am a better person than I used to be." Accompany your affirmation with the following actions.

Nix negative judgments. You and your spouse handled your marriage in such a way that placed it in its current precarious situation. You produced a result. Calling this result a "failure" is a judgment. By halting judgment, you'll be able to release the guilt of contributing to your marriage crisis. You'll be able to step out of the situation in order to learn from your past and present experiences.

Eliminating negative judgments might be challenging at first, but if you are steadfast in your awareness of these judgments and immediately replace them with positive affirmations, you'll find the task easier each time. You'll reach a point at which not judging negatively becomes part of your mind's programming.

Grow. Thousands of poems and books have been written about growing from challenges. However, even if deep in your heart you know this is true, you probably wish you had avoided the breakdown of your marriage. I felt the same way. It was only when I accepted that my husband was gone, and when I assumed responsibility for my contribution to my own reality that I was able to progress. In fact, the period of greatest personal and spiritual growth in my life occurred during my initial separation.

Instead of blaming external factors or your spouse's behavior for your own behavior, realize that somehow you aligned yourself with what happened to your marriage. It might be too late for your marriage to be saved, but it's not too late for you to save yourself.

Help others grow. If you're given the opportunity, share what you're learning with others. Sharing what you've learned does not mean lecturing or proselytizing, but to have an attitude of giving. By giving, you'll be acting like God acts. The universe will most likely provide you with chances to help others who are or might be going through similar experiences. If the people in your life need company, spend time with them. If they need someone to listen, give them your undivided attention. If they request your advice, offer it.

I made a difference in the lives of my support group friends by sharing my experience. I was able to help because these people, defying cultural, age, and geographical differences, felt what I was feeling and had spouses who behaved like my husband. On a spiritual level, I was accomplishing two things: connecting with others and serving others. I was connecting to my Highest Self by giving of myself to others.

Another interesting story is how I met one of my new (and now closest) friends. She was married to one of my husband's college friends, and had invited me and my husband for lunch. I nearly cancelled because my husband had already expressed his desire to move out, and I wasn't in the mood to socialize. But something inside drove me to go. I felt compelled to stay in touch with the wife of my husband's friend after that initial meeting, and months later, I was surprised to learn that she was going through a similar experience to mine. Being a "veteran" of the subject, I was able to give her the support and comfort she needed. I have no doubt that our meeting was by divine appointment.

Deepen your connections. When your marriage is in trouble, you might tend to avoid personal conversations or even seeing friends and family. The reason is that the illusory part of you that thinks your worth depends on your reputation fears you'll be labeled as a "failure."

Even though this is far from true, you might feel as though you're the only person in your circle of family and friends who is experiencing or has experienced marital problems.

I urge you to be aware that by forging deep connections with others, you'll be connecting with your Highest Self.

Having gone through the experience of separation and divorce helped me relate to others who had experienced severe loss or pain in their lives. Also, when I opened my heart and reached out to friends and family members for support, I was able to deepen my connection with them in ways I had never experienced before. In general, people want to help. Trust this truth and act upon it.

Tap into the abundant resources that are available to you. While you were solely focused on the breakdown of your marriage, you probably neglected meeting new people or trying new activities; but those people and activities were always there—and still are. Your new best friend is out there, eager for you to get out and meet him or her. Your new favorite hobby is waiting for your discovery.

Even though I was in pain emotionally, I made myself try new activities, such as hiking and stand up paddleboarding, which I absolutely loved. I met new people who had similar interests, and who became my new group of friends.

The past is behind you. It's time to move forward with the lessons you have learned.

"I Am Forgiving"

You're probably grappling with your ability to forgive your spouse and anyone else who, in your mind, was responsible for the breakdown of your marriage.

What exactly is forgiveness?

Forgiveness is an act of kindness toward yourself. Forgiveness does not mean:

- Forgetting what happened.
- Condoning hurtful behavior.
- Being a doormat.
- Sacrificing yourself for others.
- Pretending everything is fine.

When you forgive, you can:

- See the innocence in those who hurt you, who have done so not out of malice, but out of ignorance. They did what they thought was best for them based on their own mental programming.
- Allow yourself to release the negative energy you hold inside.
- Learn from what happened so you are not subject to similar situations in the future.
- Be happy in the present moment.
- Eliminate fear about the past repeating itself in the future.

My suggestions on how to forgive focus on raising your awareness of the following three truths.

Truth 1: Not forgiving only hurts those who can't forgive. Your spouse is not hurting because you can't forgive. You are the one with the heart palpitations, or the ulcer, or the sleeping problems. You are the one who feels increasingly bitter with each passing day. You're punishing yourself for somebody else's behavior.

Truth 2: Blame is a precursor of the need to forgive. If you need to forgive, you must have blamed. You might blame your spouse for the breakdown of your marriage or for leaving you without apparent concern for you or your children. You are likely to be unaware of the negative emotions and difficulties your spouse might be experiencing by his or her decision to leave and say, "Hey, I'm not perfect, but I really didn't do anything so awful. My spouse is the one who left me/cheated on me/abused me."

By blaming someone for your unhappiness, you are:

- *Giving up control of your life to the people who hurt you.* Their behavior determines whether you can function or not.
- *Avoiding responsibility for your own actions and feelings.* No one, and remember this, *no one* can make you feel anything. You're the only person responsible for your own feelings. By assigning blame, you don't need to deal with the responsibility, and can wait for the other person to give you permission to feel good again.
- *Settling comfortably in the role of a victim, which might grant attention from those around you.* You'll justify all the negative feelings you might be experiencing, and by doing so you'll be anchoring yourself to the past.

Truth 3: Where there is blame, there is anger. Blame not only causes the need to forgive, but also precedes anger. As you have already learned, anger has a strong pull to negative energy fields. The fog of anger can make you blind to the truth. Anger can make it impossible for you to see beauty. Beauty is God and God is beauty, so you won't be able to see God.

What to do? All it takes is a change of thought to get rid of the blame and instead take ownership of your current situation. Once you make your reality *yours*, you'll have the power to change it. Realize that no matter how angry you are, your emotions will have no impact on your spouse's past, present, or future actions. As Anthony de Mello says in *The Way to Love*, "You must drop your false belief that people can sin in awareness. Sin occurs, not, as we mistakenly think, in malice, but in ignorance."[4] Choose to see your spouse as someone who did and is doing whatever he or she thinks is best given his or her personal perceptions.

Not blaming is an expression of self-love, because you'll be saying no to a behavior that will ultimately hurt you.

Having said this, you might have times when anger still gets the best of you. That happened to me. A lot. But anger doesn't always need to have negative consequences. Anger sometimes functions as a springboard to get you out of grief and apathy, and spurs you into positive action. Being angry might help you decide to finally go out with your friends, or take on a new exercise program, or do whatever you denied yourself in the past "just to show" your spouse. In this case, anger can be a good thing. On David Hawkins's 0–1,000 scale of human consciousness, anger calibrates below the 200 level, which corresponds to negative energies, but it also calibrates at a much higher level of energy than grief. So by being angry, you are actually bumping yourself up to higher energy levels, and preparing to rise above the 200 level (into the fields of positive, empowering emotions).

When is anger negative? When it stirs you to take action against your spouse, the person your spouse was or is romantically involved with, or even against yourself. Anger can be paralyzing, and can limit your ability to reach your highest potential. When I experienced angry thoughts, I allowed myself to be angry for a while, and then immersed myself in uplifting books, meditation, spiritual CDs or movies, and prayer. At first, I would resist the positive messages, but as I continued to submerge myself in them, the racing thoughts in my head slowed down and were replaced with thoughts of forgiveness and love. Without knowing it, I was reprogramming my subconscious mind, a goal that we'll study in more depth later in this book.

A good analogy for the reprogramming process is how it feels to do a running workout. During the first few minutes, you might feel like getting off the treadmill and leaving the gym, but after you've gone past a certain threshold, you want to keep moving. This is similar to what happens when you repeatedly expose yourself to messages with positive energy: You learn to respond in different ways to the same stimuli. Light dissolves darkness by virtue of its own existence.

Another strategy in eliminating stubborn anger is to surround yourself with objects that have high energy. How do you know they emanate high energy? Because you feel good when you're around them. Think of a picture, poem, quote, or whatever else makes you smile when you see it or read it. Laminate images of this type and position them in visible places around your living space. When I was feeling my lowest, I would glance at a quote from Wayne Dyer that I had written on my white eraser board: "When you change the way you look at things, the things you look at change."[5] The message would immediately trigger a positive shift in my feelings.

"I Am Giving"

You might recall all the terrible things your spouse did, and all the pain you went and are going through, and demand justice. You want life to be fair, and in your eyes, it isn't being fair to you. You might feel peace is unattainable when life is so unfair.

I encourage you to realize that your attachment to fairness is the result of your cultural programming. Think about it: One of the first complaints you made as a kid probably was, "It's not fair!" You wanted the last piece of cake to be divided up evenly. You wanted to have the same treatment that was granted to your siblings and classmates.

Justice is "right," and anything other than a 50/50 split is "unfair." However, labeling something as "right," "wrong," "fair" or "unfair" is judgment, and judgment is driven by the ego. Considered to be the father of existentialism, Søren Kierkegaard said, "Once you label me, you negate me."[6]

Let's further explore judgment and its dreadful child: revenge.

Judgment. Eliminating all judgment is not possible for most people, because the human brain works by judging. You use the information you've gathered with your senses, assess a situation, and make a judgment. Judgment becomes problematic when it leads to negative emotions. Catch yourself when you're making a negative judgment, and try to put yourself in your spouse's shoes. Did your spouse have an affair? To your spouse, going outside the marriage seemed justifiable at the time based on his or her judgment of the situation. Your spouse was and still is a victim of his or her own judgment. This does not mean you have to be a victim, too, especially if playing the role of a victim is robbing you of the opportunity to be happy.

Revenge. When negative judgments are not controlled, they develop into anger and hatred. Demanding revenge usually follows. People whose spouses leave might want to tarnish their spouses' reputations by telling everyone what their spouses did to wrong them. They might hire tough lawyers to fight for what they "deserve." They might even entertain thoughts of emotionally or physically injuring their spouses. Some people act on these thoughts, and that's when revenge is materialized.

The desire for revenge seems alluring because it allows you to have a goal: something to strive for and to distract you from the pain you are experiencing. Also, when you pursue revenge you feel more in control because at least you're taking charge to make things "right." The flaw in this thinking is twofold: First, during and after the achievement of revenge, you'll be consumed by negative thoughts, so your negative thoughts will still paralyze you and prevent you from living life to the fullest. Second, you won't really be in control, but rather you'll be controlled by your desire to get revenge.

If you find yourself at a point in which you are acting out your desire for revenge, stop. Just like that: *Stop*. Remind yourself that by seeking revenge, you are seeking self-destruction. As the Chinese proverb says, "He who seeks vengeance, must dig two graves: one for his enemy and one for himself."[7]

A great way to weaken the desire for revenge is to practice giving for its own sake. The recipient of your gift doesn't have to be your spouse. Offer babysitting for the neighbors, or assist your parents with their yard work. Sign up for volunteering opportunities in which you can meet other people aligned with giving. Giving or even witnessing the act of giving will positively impact your serotonin (feel-good hormone) levels, and will immediately raise you to higher fields of energy.

"I Am Renewed"

When you are renewed, you are using this challenge in your life as a springboard to create positive change rather than as the precursor of guilt.

In *Power vs. Force*, David Hawkins provides scientific proof that guilt and shame are two of the lowest forms of energy on the planet, and are the closest to spiritual death. Similar to experiencing any low-energy emotions, feeling guilty about the breakdown of your marriage won't lead to different results. Instead, guilt will rob you of the self-love and self-respect that are necessary for you to heal.

I went through countless blame/guilt cycles: I would switch from blaming my husband's actions for the end of our marriage to feeling guilty for influencing his negative behavior to blaming him again.

How to turn guilt around and become renewed? There are two means of action.

First, use guilt as a propeller to figure out your role in the breakdown of the marriage. Even if you think your share of the problem is only 10 percent of the total, focus on this 10 percent, and think of ways in which you can change your negative behaviors. Aim to become not only a better partner, but a better person.

Second, treat yourself. You can nullify the guilt you feel for "blowing it" by doing what you would normally call overindulging. Why? Because by seeking renewal through pleasure, you're showing yourself love; and self-love is the antidote to the venom of guilt. Start tracking what gives you pleasure. When I put together my list, I had to stop writing. I didn't stop because I had run out of ideas, but because I couldn't wait to start enjoying the items on my list. Here is a sample of my pleasure list:

- Wrapping myself up in a warm blanket in the winter.
- Savoring a bowl of ice cream topped with brownies.
- Cycling on a crisp autumn morning.
- Having my hair braided.
- Buying a new outfit that looks amazing on me.

- Singing and dancing to my favorite song.
- Going to the aquarium or to the zoo.
- Playing with a child.
- Laughing.
- Feeding the goats at the local farm.
- Going for a walk in the woods.
- Curling up with a good book.
- Petting a puppy.
- Getting a massage.

You get the idea. Write your own list and keep it handy. When guilt strikes you, pull out the list and follow through on one of its suggestions.

"I Am Now"

This means what you might have heard a million times, but have forgotten: The only moment available to you is now. Being in the now immediately eliminates regret, because regret is nothing more than attachment to the past.

You might wish you could change the past, but wishing will only be a waste of your present time. Embrace your past experiences for the lessons that they taught you, and then discard them for good.

The best way to nullify regret and live fully in the now is to develop a constant awareness. Catch yourself when you find yourself reminiscing about the past and wishing things were different, and switch your focus to the present moment. A powerful strategy to be in the now is to focus on what your senses perceive. Be conscious of being alive. Try to discern every instrument in a song, describe the scents around you, slide the tips of your fingers over surfaces of varying roughness, or chew your food slowly and with purpose. You must love yourself to be able to do this, because living in the now is another form of self-love.

Also, I invite you to consider the concept of time. You might have heard that time is an illusion, and that the past, present, and future happen simultaneously, a concept that is difficult to grasp in a culture built on linearity. If the past is an illusion, your feelings of regret are based on an illusion. You'll have the power to be rid of regret because you'll be aware that regret has no real basis to exist. The only way to get in touch with the illusory concept of time is by meditating. When you make conscious contact with God, time seems to dissolve into joy. Meditating can be challenging at first, especially if you have preconceived notions about the "right" way to meditate. Even so, with practice and determination, you can make it an integral part of your life. I invite you to use the mantra, "I am now" in your meditation practice. I'll talk further on meditation when I address your connection with your divine nature and also in Chapter 14 of this book.

"I Am Safe"

Uncertainty, which is an outgrowth of your perception of stability in your life, will have no power over you if you become aware that you have never stopped being safe.

Being paralyzed by uncertainty is being paralyzed by fear of the unknown. In *A Course in Miracles*, the truth is clearly stated: "If you knew Who walks beside you on the way that you have chosen, fear would be impossible."[8] There's no need to fear the unknown, because if you're steadfast in your alignment with the energies of your Highest Self, you'll be guided to where you are intended to go.

During my initial separation from my husband, my stomach would clench into painful spasms every time I thought about the future. Nothing was "certain" in my mind anymore. I believed that being with my husband was "safe." I had him, my in-laws, and a place in society. I felt financially secure because we could depend on each other. If a tragedy happened to me, my husband would be there to rescue me. Certainty in life was one of my requirements to being at peace.

What I didn't realize is that my perception of certainty was just that: a perception.

Francois de La Rochefoucauld said, "The only thing constant in life is change."[9] Every second in the future of our linear continuum brings billions of possibilities, and the result that is manifested depends on your subconscious alignment.

Certainty is an illusion, and the only unchangeable entity in the universe is God. In *Three Magic Words* by Uell S. Andersen, this truth is revealed: "Only the great unity—your own association with the infinite, your own individual manifestation of the universal mind of God—only that is changeless."[10]

To change your perception about uncertainty, I suggest the following three-step process.

Step 1: See the reality of your situation. Stepping out of the situation and seeing it from the perspective of a witness was very helpful to me. I invite you to jot down the most important aspects of your life that are changing and, in the most objective way possible, contemplate the potential impact of these changes. To achieve maximum objectivity, a good strategy is to pretend you're writing about a stranger who's facing a situation similar to yours.

When I was in pain, I wrote down some of the areas in her life where a woman transitioning from married to single is likely to undergo changes. These include:

- *Marital status.* She will check the single box on forms and tax documents. When people ask if she's married, she'll answer no.
- *Location.* If she moved after her divorce, she'll meet new neighbors and take a different way to work. Depending on her financial situation, she might have less physical space in which to live. She might not have to share her living space with anyone except for her children, if she has them.

- *Children.* Depending on her child custody arrangement, she might change some of her and her children's daily routines. She might have to spend time away from her children.
- *Career.* She might have to change jobs or career fields to meet her new financial needs. She might have a new manager, new coworkers, and a different commute.
- *Income.* She'll likely have less household income. Her expenses will be lower as well.
- *Relationship with in-laws and common friends.* She might choose to continue a positive relationship with the in-laws who express their willingness to stay in touch. She might lose some friends and strengthen her connection with others.

As soon as I finished the list, it dawned on me that this woman was me. And then I felt empowered to take on the changes. For if I hadn't known this woman, I wouldn't have thought the upcoming changes in her life were unbearable.

Regardless of your specific circumstances, this exercise will help you gain a less biased perspective on your situation.

Step 2: Visualize joy in the future. The future is a blank canvas, and you may choose to see this unpainted canvas as a cause for anxiety or as a means to exploring exciting possibilities.

I suggest you visualize a joyful future because the other option is to visualize a miserable future, and you know that when you place all your energy on what you don't want, you'll get more of what you don't want.

When I did my visualization, I created detailed and vivid images in my head, which would translate into a feeling of peace and eventually, elation. During this visualization process I wasn't daydreaming; I was *assuming the feeling of the wish fulfilled,* which is Neville Goddard's main premise in *The Power of Awareness,* as well as a concept we'll explore in depth in Chapter 10.

I also gave form to my vision of the future by creating lists that triggered positive, uplifting feelings inside of me, including a list of:

- Things that I felt grateful for.
- My top 100 accomplishments.
- New experiences and new people in my life.
- Ways my friends and relatives support me.
- My values.
- Experiences I want to have in the future.
- Places to visit.
- Inspiring activities or people.

I suggest you create your own lists, and picture a future that might be uncertain, but promises to be wonderful.

Step 3: Remember where you came from. When you focus on the uncertainty of your future, you forget your divine nature. If you remember your immutable connection to Spirit, you'll receive divine guidance.

This was the most powerful strategy for me, because instead of focusing on my desired earthly accomplishments, I placed my energy on the only entity that is real: Spirit. In between bouts of anxiety and fear, I prayed. And I always received an answer that manifested itself in both expected and unexpected ways. I assumed that everything would work out in my best interest and that the right people would show up in my life.

How did I put this strategy in action? I needed to sell my house and move to a less expensive place, so I followed my intuition to select a real estate agent from the list in the newspaper. This agent found a new home for me in the perfect location, and next to amazingly helpful neighbors. Through my writing and radio show hosting, I was guided to meet an amazing group of like-minded people who encouraged me to pursue my calling to help others. I reached out to my in-laws and was able to renew my connection with the few who chose to remain part of my life. I followed my intuition when selecting which events and activities to participate in, and created a new circle of friends who knew me as a single person. Life appeared to be safer and more stable, but I reminded myself that I had been safe all along.

Repeat, "I am safe," in moments of uncertainty, and trust that divine guidance will come to you.

"I Am with My Senior Partner"

People who haven't gone through your experience will tell you that if you are lonely, all you need to do is call a friend or go to the movies. They cannot empathize with your persistent feelings of loneliness regardless of the identity or the number of people who are with you.

Dissolving your feelings of loneliness is a three-step process, one that will evolve at the pace you decide.

Step 1: Become comfortable with yourself. This is essential for your emotional readiness to appreciate the company of other people.

Becoming comfortable with who you are requires self-love. Founder of Hay House and motivational author Louise Hay often says in her lectures that you'll have a relationship with yourself your whole life, so you'd better learn to like yourself. When you love yourself, you'll feel that you are in the best company when you are alone.

During the worst part of my journey through marital separation, I was too frazzled to see my own magnificence. Evenings were the most challenging, and I'd find myself driving to the mall after work just to be surrounded by other people. Unfortunately, my mall escapades didn't provide relief because the low energies that were consuming me were blocking my connection with my Highest Self.

I encourage you to meditate on the precious gift that you are. Consider all the amazing qualities you possess, and all the love you have inside. You can also connect with your Highest Self through listening to music, painting, taking walks in nature, or any other activity that brings you joy. Every time you're so consciously aware of the present moment that time seems to fly, you're connected with who you really are.

Once you feel comfortable in your own company, seek the company of people who love you and care about you.

Step 2: Appreciating the company of other people. I wasn't able to see the gift of other people's company throughout the time of my separation. I thought that only my husband was capable of taking away the hollow feeling in my stomach. I materialized my constant thoughts about loneliness by remaining lonely. As I grew spiritually, I learned that the physical presence or absence of my husband had absolutely no power over me unless I decided to give it power. I also increased my awareness of the people around me, and realized that they were spending part of their precious time on this planet with me. By adopting a different perspective, I started to appreciate people more and to be grateful for their presence.

Don't seek others' company as a subconscious way to establish new emotional attachments, because as soon as these people are not physically with you, your sense of loneliness will return.

Finally, when you have company, it might be tempting to talk about your miserable situation nonstop, but then you'll be wasting those moments with people who want you by their side talking about someone who didn't want you by his or her side. You'll attract more of what is, or more of what you don't want.

Step 3: Realize you are never truly alone. Every second before, during, and after your incarnation on Earth, God has been, is, and will be with you. God is like a senior partner who will never leave your side. God does not judge you, and loves you in a way beyond human comprehension. You are a magnificent expression of God's creation, and the spark of God is within you. You are already connected to the Divine within; all you need to do now is to realize that connection.

The Prayer of Saint Francis ties all of the aforementioned *I am* affirmations together.

> *Lord, make me an instrument of your peace,*
> *Where there is hatred, let me sow love;*
> *Where there is injury, pardon;*
> *Where there is doubt, faith;*
> *Where there is despair, hope;*
> *Where there is darkness, light;*

Where there is sadness, joy.
O Divine Master,
Grant that I may not so much seek to be consoled, as to console;
To be understood, as to understand;
To be loved, as to love.
For it is in giving that we receive,
It is in pardoning that we are pardoned,
And it is in dying that we are born to Eternal Life.

Saint Francis not only dissolves low energy feelings through the light of his divine connection; he asks to serve so he can be "born to Eternal Life," which I interpret as having a clean connection with Spirit.

I suggest that when you find yourself aligning with low-energy emotions, you ask yourself, "How may I be of service to others?" When we give, we do the only thing that God can do. And if we behave like God, we are immediately lifted to higher levels of energy and positive emotions. Start your journey by being aware, nullify the low energies with higher energies and, when you're ready, start giving.

CHAPTER 4

Using Your Life's Currency
The Law of Attraction

"The assumption of the wish fulfilled is the ship that carries
you over the unknown seas to the fulfillment of your dream."
—Neville Goddard

You're probably spending a huge chunk of your time and energy ruminating on your current marriage situation. If you're separated, you might be analyzing what went wrong and fighting even the thought of not sharing your life with your spouse anymore. If you're currently going through, or have already gone through, a divorce, you might still be analyzing, fighting, and wallowing in low energies at the realization that your marriage is over. Your time investment, however, is producing zero returns. Your spouse is still gone. You're putting all your energy (your life's currency) on what you don't want, and the universe responds to you by providing you with more of what you don't want.

It's time to talk about the Law of Attraction.

The Law of Attraction

Thomas Troward was one of the first New Thought authors to introduce the Law of Attraction, but it wasn't until 2006 that *The*

Secret by Rhonda Byrne made this law accessible and popular. However, many people misunderstood the message of *The Secret*, and thought that it meant they could materialize the things or the people they "needed" in order to be happy. See the flaw? If you're applying the Law of Attraction to get your spouse back or to attract a new romantic relationship because you believe you *need* romantic love to be happy, you're approaching the situation from the perspective of the false self (the ego), who believes your happiness is dependent on exterior circumstances.

What is the true meaning of the Law of Attraction?

For me, the Law of Attraction represents the impact the universe has on your life in direct response to your self-identity.

As Uell Andersen expresses in *Three Magic Words,* "There is no escaping this wheel of answered thought and belief."[1] If you're anxiously focusing on how to get your spouse back, it's likely that you'll receive more anxiety in return. If you think about wanting peace because you don't have it, you're conveying lack of peace to the universe and will continue receiving more of the same. Finally, if you think that you need a mate to be happy, you're telling the universe that you are unhappy, so you will attract unhappiness.

You don't need your spouse in your life to be happy. In fact, you don't need to be married to anyone to be happy. You only need to be happy first to attract happiness.

The seemingly paradoxical concept of being happy to attract happiness is expressed by philosophical author James Allen: "A man can only attract to him which is in harmony with his nature."[2] If you are happy, you'll feed happiness to the universe, and in return, you'll receive more happiness. By spending all your time feeling sad, angry, afraid, and guilty, you're not only wasting your precious present moments, you're also ensuring that the cause of your damaging emotions will continue showing up in your life.

If we had to define the root cause of happiness, it would be love. God is love and love is God, so by being love, you're connecting to your Highest Self. Once you have reached this connection, there's no place for unhappiness. When you clean your connection to the Divine, your unhappiness dissolves instantaneously.

How to apply the Law of Attraction to love? If you are being love, you will extend love to others, including your spouse, and then love will be returned to you.

How to Be Love

Being love simply is being who you really are. Your true self, your Highest Self, is pure love because, as we said before, God is love and God is in you.

It can't be so simple, you might think. That's your ego resisting the truth that will set you free.

My road to be love was bumpy because of my ego. At the beginning of my journey, I did all the time-wasting I could physically allow myself to do. I spent countless nights awake, reliving the past, trying to come up with answers to save my marriage, and worrying about my uncertain future. I spent days misplacing and losing things as important as my passport, leaving doors unlocked at night, and forgetting business appointments. My grief became so extreme that I feared I would never be able to recover. I only wanted my life to end. Quickly.

After one episode of grief subsided, I would wallow in regret for wasting my youth in a marriage that ended. Regret would trigger more grief, which would trigger another episode of regret. It was a vicious cycle that only stopped when I made the conscious choice to be who I really was. I *remembered* I was one with God, and by remembering, I became love.

Practical suggestions for being love are:

- Before going to sleep and immediately upon awakening, say the following words with *intention*: "I am love. Love is already in my life." I stress the word *intention* because if you only say the words without spiritually connecting with your words, you'll be acting like a parrot. In my case, practicing this affirmation materialized as an outpouring of support from old and new friends.

- Take note of the positive impact you have on the world and on other people's lives. Give yourself a pat on the back for your kindness.
- See your true beauty when you look in the mirror and appreciate the myriad miracles that happen in your body without your conscious intervention: your heart beating, your lungs breathing, and your liver and kidneys detoxifying you.
- Smile at strangers. Most people will smile back! However, don't be attached to the need to receive smiles in return, or your false self will be the one smiling.
- Look for opportunities to serve and to be kind. Pay the toll for the person behind you in traffic. Pick up litter during your walks. Offer a compliment to the receptionist at the doctor's office.
- Express gratitude. Call your parents just to thank them for raising you. Tell your kids how grateful you are for their hugs. Give thanks when you come to a traffic light that immediately turns green. Appreciate the bed you sleep in every night. Thank God for the warm rays of the sun on your skin.
- Send love to your spouse regardless of your spouse's previous actions. If you no longer have contact with him or her, send love through daily prayer. By treating my husband as kindly and lovingly as I could, I was able to connect with him at a level that allowed us to part ways in peace.

How to Be Lucky

You might be thinking that being love to attract love—and as a result, to attract happiness—is just a game of luck. You might think that even though you've always been kind and giving, people like your spouse take advantage of your generosity and walk all over you.

If this is your affirmation, the universe's response to you will be to continue providing you with situations in which you end up being a doormat. That's the Law of Attraction at work.

Luck is the direct result of being aware. Lucky people are not special. The lucky ones are in tune with their Highest Selves, and are able to use their intuition (divine guidance) to know where to go and who to meet. Intuition is contact made by the conscious mind with the subconscious mind, which holds the collective wisdom shared by all human beings. We'll explore the difference between your conscious and your subconscious mind in future chapters, in which we'll study the concept of the ego and the power of your imagination.

A simple, everyday example that illustrates the role of awareness in your luck is the selection of a new car. Let's say you and your neighbor have both decided to purchase new cars. You have a good idea of what you want, but are unsure whether model A is better than model B. You wake up, and turn on the TV. You tune out the traffic news and the weather report, but listen intently when a commercial for model A comes up. During your morning drive, the roads seem flooded with the two models you're considering, and you realize model A looks better from the back. You have a doctor's appointment at lunch, and while you wait, you spot a magazine with consumer report information that shows better gas mileage for model A. You're leaning toward model A, but are still not sure what to do, so you ask the person sitting next to you for his opinion. The guy turns out to be a car salesman, and offers you a great deal on model A.

You go home and tell your neighbor what happened. Your neighbor says you're lucky. He's been worried about not being able to find the right car for weeks, and his prophecy is self-fulfilled: His junky old car is still parked in his driveway. The truth is that your neighbor has been too distracted by his negative thoughts to notice the signs that would've guided him to the best choice. The abundance of the universe was there all along, and your awareness allowed you to tap into this abundance of knowledge and wisdom.

Is there such thing as bad luck?

Bad luck is the result of placing your awareness on what you don't want. If you spend night and day thinking about the trauma of your separation or divorce, or about how wrecked your life will be, all you'll notice are the low energies around you. You'll focus on the tailgaters on the road, the rude people on the street, and the kids who are having screaming tantrums. Chances are the low energies around you will be compounded with yours, so maybe you'll trip and fall, or have a car accident. You'll say to yourself, "It's my bad luck," which is another affirmation that will result in more of the same "bad luck."

Choose to be lucky.

PART TWO

From Ego to Your Highest Self

CHAPTER 5

Your Highest Self vs. Your Ego
Always a Winning Battle

*"Spiritual vision literally cannot see error, and merely looks
for Atonement. All solutions the spiritual eye seeks dissolve."*
—*A Course in Miracles*

To align your thoughts and actions with those of your Highest Self, you need to clearly understand how your Highest Self differs from the ego.

The Ego

The part of you that is real only in your perception, but drives you to embark on a never-ending search for satisfaction and meaning through worldly things, activities, or people is called the *ego.* If we rearrange the letters in the word *ego,* we get *geo,* a Greek prefix meaning "earth." The ego is anchored to the earthly realm. The ego is your false self.

By definition, the ego is in direct opposition to your connection with your Highest Self, because the ego is based on duality and separateness, and your Highest Self cannot be divided. During separation or divorce, how does the polarity between the ego and your Highest Self express itself? Take a look at this chart comparing the two.

The Ego . . .	Your Highest Self . . .
Drives you to sink into low-energy levels when you learn that your marriage is in trouble or is ending.	Remains at the highest level of energy no matter your life circumstances.
Tells you that you're destined to be alone for the rest of your life.	Knows nothing about loneliness because it's always connected to God and to others.
Deplores your life circumstances without your spouse. To the ego, happiness is impossible without a romantic partner.	Doesn't judge your life circumstances, but sees them as they are. Your Highest Self doesn't need anything or anyone to be happy, because it is, and has always been, happy.
Fights your current situation and insists you can act to reverse the breakdown of your marriage.	Knows that everything happens in divine order, including the state of your marriage.
Tries to control your spouse's actions because it thinks that your happiness depends on your spouse's behavior. If you're unsuccessful in controlling your spouse, you feel unworthy and bitter toward everyone around you.	Knows that people, including your spouse, are free to do as they like without impacting the love you have for yourself and for others.
Thinks that you are a victim of your life circumstances.	Assumes responsibility for your life circumstances because it knows that you were aligned, either consciously or subconsciously, with the current and past events in your life.

The descriptions above illustrate the main elements of the ego that manifest in your current situation. These are:

- Disconnection.
- Attachment.
- Resistance.
- Blaming.

Your Highest Self

Your Highest Self is the closest you can be to your inner divinity. Your Highest Self has always been connected to everything and everyone in the universe, including your spouse. Your Highest Self has no past because it only exists in the now. Your Highest Self is complete without the need to achieve anything or to be married to anyone. Your Highest Self doesn't judge any situation, but accepts the current circumstances in your life as they are.

Your Highest Self is infinite, and has access to the ocean of abundance found within God's creations, including the abundance of love. Your Highest Self is all-knowing, and is capable of accessing the wisdom embedded in universal human consciousness. Your Highest Self is pure, unconditional love, so nothing other than love can emanate from it. Your Highest Self is the only constant, never-changing element in your life and in the universe. Your Highest Self is more than happiness; it's indescribable *bliss*.

In order to heal and clean your connection to your Highest Self, you must replace the elements of the ego mentioned before with:

- Connection.
- Detachment.
- Allowing.
- Owning.

In the following chapters, you'll learn how to tame the elements of the ego through connection with your Highest Self.

CHAPTER 6

Disconnection to Connection
Going Where You Belong

"We cannot live only for ourselves. A thousand fibers
connect us with our fellow men; and among those
fibers, as sympathetic threads, our actions run as
causes, and they come back to us as effects."
—Herman Melville

When you're ruled by your false self while going through separation or divorce, you will not only feel disconnected from your spouse, but also from everyone else, from love, and even from God. Your sense of separateness drives you away from where you belong: a place of unadulterated connectedness with everything and everyone in the universe.

Connecting to God:
The Ego's View

A sense of disconnection from God automatically blocks your connection with your Highest Self, where true happiness resides. As *A Course in Miracles* says, the "only lack we need to correct is the sense of separation from God."[1]

Conceptualizing God as an external mystical force is part of our cultural programming. God is portrayed as a bearded white male in a white robe looking down from the sky. This ego-designed god keeps track of people who are naughty or nice. He's angry when people sin and is pleased when people make sacrifices in his name. He whimsically favors some people and abandons others. He grants earthly wishes, such as making the rain stop so you can go for a run or opening your spouse's eyes to see what he or she is missing by leaving you.

If your marriage is breaking down and you perceive yourself as separate from God, you'll see God as someone who has also abandoned you while you suffer the greatest loss in your life.

When you feel abandoned by God, your emotional state will remain in the lowest energy fields. Your emotions will fluctuate from shame to fear to anger to anxiety. You'll always feel alone, even if you're surrounded by people who are kind and loving toward you. You'll start devaluing life, seeing it as meaningless. You'll lose hope. Your hopelessness will strengthen your perception of separateness and will result in a perpetual cycle of low-energy emotions.

You might also blame God for what happened to you, and try to find the reasons for this apparent punishment. If you discover God's "reasons" to punish you, you'll be plagued by guilt and regret. If you can't find any reasons for your punishment, you'll experience frustration and anger at the unfairness of the situation.

By blaming anything external to you, including your ego-created image of God, for your current situation, you're avoiding responsibility. If you evade responsibility, you're also relinquishing the power to change the circumstances in your life.

This situation can be turned around by accessing the power of your Highest Self.

Connecting to God:
Your Highest Self's View

God is the complete absence of ego. Low-energy emotions are not the emotions of God. Why? Because negative emotions need duality to exist (paradigms of sad-happy, anxious-peaceful, angry-calm), and God is the opposite of duality. Furthermore, you are a divine creation. Within you exists a spark of God. This means you are not and have never been disconnected from God. All you have to do to extricate yourself from pain is to clean your existing connection with God. A clean connection to the Divine requires:

- *Awareness*, because once you see the truth you can be your Highest Self.
- *Silence*, because you'll be able to communicate with God more easily when you're able to quiet your mind.
- *Giving*, because all God does is give, and by giving, you're being God-like.

Awareness

We have already touched on the subject of awareness, but let's delve into it a little further. Awareness means being attentive to your divine nature as you go about your day-to-day activities. This will allow you to "catch yourself" every time you have an ego-driven thought, and prevent the negative emotions and actions associated with these thoughts from manifesting in your life.

Being aware of egotistical thoughts will become more natural to you as you grow spiritually and heal emotionally. You'll adopt a subconscious alarm bell that will go off every time you have a low-energy thought. When the alarm sounds, you'll replace the thought with its high-energy counterpart. It's important to reframe as soon as you catch yourself, before the thought causes negative emotions within you.

I've been working on sharpening my sense of awareness for a long time, but out-of-the-blue low-energy thoughts still come to me at times. I can be driving, or cooking, or sitting in a movie theatre, and a negative thought about my loss will pop up. I've become skilled at quickly telling myself that I will not waste a moment in my life dwelling on what I don't want or what I don't like. Then, I replace the negative thought with a thought that uplifts and nourishes my soul. I know I'm making progress because the low-energy thoughts come to me less often now, and I'm able to tame them more easily.

There will be times when awareness seems impossible or simply not welcome, such as the days immediately before or after your divorce date, or on your wedding anniversary. Sometimes you might feel as though you *want* to be sad, angry, or regretful. If negative thoughts and emotions seem to be too difficult to overcome, or if you choose not to overcome them at the moment, then let them be and patiently wait for them to be dissolved by the light of your divine being.

Awareness not only means to be attentive, but also to be fully in the now, where Spirit resides.

How to regain an awareness of the now? First, fill your mind with information on the subject by reading books such as *The Power of Now* by Eckhart Tolle and *The Power of Intention* by Wayne Dyer. Once you've internalized the information you've gathered, apply the following strategies every time you notice your mind drifting away from the present moment.

- *Fully concentrate on something tangible around you.* For example, if you're driving, run your fingers along the steering wheel and pay attention to the texture and temperature of the material. During a walk, focus on one of the sounds around you, such as the sound of a chirping bird. By fully engaging your senses in the now, you'll be conscious that you are a living being, and will bring your mind to the present moment.
- *Imagine yourself disengaging from your body and hovering over it.* Notice your body's position, posture, and physical

qualities. By practicing this, you will not only regain awareness, but a different perspective on your behavior at the moment.

Silence

As the American novelist and poet Herman Melville said, "Silence is the only Voice of our God."[2] Try listening to God's voice while watching the nightly news or while wallowing in self-pity. You'll only hear the TV or your ego. It's in silence, free of these distractions, when you can listen to your own internal voice, which is the voice of God. From what I've learned, being in silence is not necessarily the same as meditating, because as you'll learn in Chapter 14, you can meditate while listening to soothing music, chanting a mantra (called Japa meditation), or going for a walk. Silent meditation will allow you to open the doors to divine wisdom.

I used to resist silence and meditation. I determined I was too busy to be quiet, and every time I tried it, I would find myself thinking about the next item on my to-do list. During my separation and divorce, grief became a new obstacle to peaceful silence. All of my thoughts and energy were focused on my situation. However, I was resolved to clean my connection with my Highest Self, so I started carving out a few minutes of my day to be in silence. As time went by, it became easier and even desirable to be in this completely quiet state.

Giving

Giving is the last piece of the God-connection puzzle. You already know that all God does is give, but I invite you to contemplate the truth of this statement in your heart. Think about this: A divine power allowed your body to come into form from a cluster of cells in your mother's womb. This intelligence also allowed you to be born and to grow. The same intelligence allows your heart to beat, your hormones to control your bodily functions, and your brain to think without the need for your direction. Has God sent you a bill for rendered services yet? Has God charged the animals and plants in nature? Our ego-created image of God demands sacrifices and strings of prayers in order to give. The true God just gives because God is love, and the only thing that can be done with love is to give it away.

Let's say you meet someone new and, during conversation, you learn that this person likes to play tennis as much as you do. It's likely that the two of you will schedule a match or a time to "hit the ball." Once you and this person realize you're alike, you form a rapport. Once you establish a rapport, you can more fully connect and become friends. The more rapport you have, the closer your connection will be, until the connection is so solid that it's able to withstand the future, inevitable life changes. This can be applied to your connection with God. If you act like God would, if you have something in common with Spirit, you'll create divine rapport, which will strengthen your divine connection.

During my darkest moments, giving of myself to others was a guaranteed source of spiritual relief. I felt a burst of happiness when providing advice to my online support group, volunteering, or doing something as simple as holding the door for people or smiling at strangers.

Giving pays off. Try it.

Connecting to Your Spouse: The Ego's View

If you feel separate from God, you'll sense disconnection from your spouse. At some point during your marriage, you probably thought your connection with your spouse was unique, because there was romantic love involved and a promise to be together "forever." I urge you to realize that a sense of connection targeted to a singular human being is egotistical in nature, because it's based on emotional attachment and not on connection to Spirit.

When an emotion is ego-driven, it eventually results in the manifestation of negative energies. The loss of the person you *"needed"* triggers all the negative emotions we studied in the first part of this book.

You might be interpreting the loss of the physical and/or emotional presence of your spouse as disconnection. You might feel as though your spouse has switched to the "other team." He or she has become your enemy. A common complaint from my fellow support group members was that their partners had turned into strangers. "He's not the person I married!" they said. I felt the same way. It seemed as though the person I had married was two different men: the one who was by my side during the first years of our marriage, and the one who decided to leave me.

Your sense of disconnection might deepen during the divorce proceedings as you and your spouse start treating your marriage as a business deal. If your spouse is greedy or ignorant about divorce laws, the financial arguments will probably be even more difficult. If you and your spouse have opposite views on child custody, you might end up playing the role of the defendant in court to "fight" for custody of your children. I remember getting stomach pangs every time I received emails from my lawyer's office, which would always be titled *Stock vs. Stock*. After sharing most of our adult lives together, my husband and I became one *versus* (against) the other.

Connecting to Your Spouse: Your Highest Self's View

Being spiritually connected to your spouse before, during, and after divorce is possible. In fact, you have always been connected, because both of you are parts of one human consciousness, and share a spark of God.

You might say that my statement above might be true, but it's too abstract, and you still feel disconnected. I understand, since your emotional attachment to your spouse is still strong.

There is hope, however.

In a moment, I'll provide you with several rational truths that you may contemplate to regain the feeling of connection with your spouse. Beware that your underlying motive isn't to get back together with your spouse, or to "be friends" after you have both gone separate ways. These motives come from the ego in its efforts to cling to its emotional attachment. The main goal is to raise your energy level so you can connect with your Highest Self.

There are other benefits to having a sense of connection with your spouse, including:

- Increased positive energy in your spouse, which benefits the energy levels of humanity as a whole.
- Increased positive energy in your children, who see their parents working together instead of fighting each other.
- Increased positive energy in your and your spouse's families, who will engage in a lot less blaming, judging, and badmouthing.
- Improved ability to co-parent.
- Smoother divorce negotiations.

Ready to regain your sense of connection? Here are some tips.

Remember that your spouse still is the person you married. His or her body, behavior, and beliefs might have changed, but your spouse's essence is the same. You and your spouse still share the same universal human consciousness, and that is immutable. Internalize this idea, and feel love pouring out from your heart toward your spouse and everyone else on the planet.

Eliminate darkness with light. When attacked, don't attack back. Take some time off from interacting with your spouse if needed, and then bring back the light through a shared positive memory.

I used this approach during my divorce negotiations. When my husband sent emails I perceived as aggressive, I gave myself time to calm down before replying. Then, I searched my memory for something good he did for me during our marriage, or something I admired about him. I communicated the memory to him in a kind and loving way. The result? Raised energy levels in both of us. Note that it's important to mean what you say or this strategy won't yield positive results. "Faked" light doesn't get rid of darkness.

Conceptualize your spouse as your teammate in business. You and your spouse are not only life partners, but business partners who share assets that are being divided. Good business partners work together to benefit the "business" of the family. Also, if you have children, you two will be co-parents. Successful co-parents need to work harmoniously for the well-being of their children. Reframe the definition of your spouse that you carry around. All of your relationships are perceptions of the mind so, by reframing your perception, you'll be changing the relationship with your spouse from toxic to healthy.

Be like water. The 43rd verse of the *Tao Te Ching* says, "The softest of all things overrides the hardest of all things. That without substance enters where there is no space."[3] What is the softest, yet paradoxically the strongest, of all things? Water. Home contractors always say, "Water damage is the worst!" What better picture of the strength of water than the work of the Colorado River to create the Grand Canyon.

Being soft yet impactful is especially important during negotiations of assets and custody of the children. In Appendix A of this book, we'll contemplate how to keep your sense of connection with your spouse intact when interacting with attorneys and when conducting negotiations.

Connecting to Other People:
The Ego's View

Your sense of disconnection might extend to all the people around you. Remember that the ego sees itself as separate from everyone else, and because of this it sees others as contenders in a fight for the best life. The resentment you may harbor toward your spouse will deepen this sense of disconnection, and it could cause you to feel unable to trust anyone.

Typical behaviors triggered by a sense of separateness range from shutting down other people to desperately seeking their attention. Can you see yourself in either of the following situations?

- *Retreating.* This involves shunning family and friends, avoiding what used to provide joy, seeking refuge in junk food, remaining in a state of grief, and feeling numb to life.
- *Taking on the role of a victim.* This includes blaming the spouse for the breakdown of the marriage, and telling everyone about it. The attention seeker will always switch the topic of conversation to the walk-away spouse and to the pain of a crumbling marriage.

During my worst days, I alternated between retreating and taking on the role of a victim. I felt like the odd woman in a sea of strangers. I didn't fit in. I felt lonely, but even so didn't feel compelled to interact with anyone. I thought that no one cared about me, and when people were kind to me, I doubted their good intentions. I complained it wasn't fair that people who had been "bad" seemed to have it better than I did. I felt jealous at the sight of couples holding hands or families seeming to enjoy an outing together. Looking back, it's hard to believe I sank so low, but I did. I wasted precious days of my life and the opportunity to connect with others by aligning myself with these low-energy levels. By perceiving myself as lonely, I remained in a state of loneliness.

Connecting to Other People: Your Highest Self's View

As Uell S. Andersen expresses in *Three Magic Words*, "We are all branches of one great tree which neither chastises itself nor destroys itself, but is simply contemplative and creative."[4] Thousands of thinkers and authors have communicated this idea of our interconnectedness using slightly different words. However, just reading that by virtue of being a divine creation you're already connected to everyone else on this planet might not help you feel any more connected. The reason is that reading or listening (knowing *about* something) isn't enough. *Feeling* and *experiencing* this connection, *knowing* in your heart that you are connected to other human beings, is essential for peace.

How do you *experience* connection? By taking action.

Don't wait for people to help you. People might not take the initiative to help you because they are afraid of coming across as intrusive, but if you reach out to them, most will provide you with love and support. Also, contact others from a position of love, not from the position of a victim, or you'll continue playing the role of a victim.

I'll outline six of the support sources I sought, which might also be beneficial to you. Add your own ways to reach out to people. Also, expand your efforts to connect with as many people as possible. If you only focus on one or two people, you might become dependent on their presence to support you, which is nothing more than switching the subject of your emotional attachment.

Regardless of the sources you choose to connect with, you'll realize that human kindness is infinitely abundant and available for you to tap into its bounty.

Support Groups

Research support groups in your local area whose meetings you can attend in person. If you don't have the time for meetings or prefer to keep your identity private, you may want to try an online support group. My online group was instrumental in my healing. Through it, I received encouragement and advice from people all over the world. Best of all, I was able to serve them by providing objective feedback. I felt joy when I stepped out of my self-centeredness to help others because I was acting like God acts, and God is pure joy. Examining other situations from an outsider's perspective taught me to look at my own situation more objectively.

There's one caveat. Because your group members will provide you with the compassion and understanding you crave, you may develop a subconscious need to remain stuck in the pain so you can continue receiving this nurturing emotional care. You may also confuse the rapport you form with a group member of the opposite sex with a romantic connection.

Many people who attend support groups believe they have found their "soul mates," when in reality they have just met people who share the pain derived from separation and divorce. A relationship based on pain will either perpetuate the pain or will fall apart when the pain goes away. Remind yourself that your ultimate goal is to let go of that pain and the need to be part of a support group.

Solution-Oriented Counselors

Seeing a counselor isn't a magic solution to "fix" your life or your marriage. While a mental health professional can help you see your situation more objectively and find solutions, a counselor who focuses on the low-energy emotions and blames your past and other people for your misery may cause more damage. This is why finding the right counselor is as important as finding the right lawyer.

I spent many hours talking to individual and marriage counselors who focused on the grief and sorrow. When I shared my negative state, they would ask, "So how does that feel?" It felt bad, of course. They would prompt me to give a voice to my pain, which turned the emotion into something tangible and real. The sessions focused on what was wrong with my marriage, and I usually would leave feeling worse about myself and about my life in general.

I eventually found a marriage coach who would agree to provide practical solutions to make my interactions with my husband positive, even if we ended up divorced. The marriage coach continued guiding me after the divorce was filed to make sure the divorce process went as smoothly as possible.

Remember that you can choose to switch counselors if the current one isn't helping you. Staying with counselors because they already know you and "it's too hard to start with someone else" is an attachment-driven excuse. Make the best of the gift of time that has been given to you.

True Friends

One of the blessings in disguise of your situation is the opportunity to determine who is and isn't a trusted friend. Some of the friends you had in common with your spouse might "pick sides," so some may disappear from your life altogether. People resist change, so if these friends have a mental picture of you and your spouse as "one," they might not know how to respond when you're not together anymore. They might stay away from you to not have to face the situation. Remind yourself that these former friends are acting the best way they can, given where they are in their own life journeys. They're not acting out of malice. You and they are connected as creations of the Divine.

You'll be able to count on the friends who choose to stay by your side. In them, you may find listening ears, helpers to manage your home and children without your spouse, and companions ready to together explore new activities. Some of your old friendships will deepen after you reach out, because by opening your heart, those friends will open their hearts to you too.

Finally, make new friends who have only met you as *you*, and not as somebody's husband or wife. These friends will help you adjust to your new social/marital status, and will not center conversations on your situation.

Family

Many of your family members will be there to support you. However, you must be especially careful not to complain to them about your spouse because they're very likely to respond to complaints with anger, desire for revenge, and judgment. You might feel temporarily relieved when "venting" to your relatives, but their low-energy emotions will eventually affect you and your children.

Your parents are the most susceptible to experiencing negative reactions, so only provide basic information to them.

In-laws

Some of your in-laws might want to stay in touch with you during your separation and after your divorce. Some of them might stop all contact as soon as they hear about your separation. Some will promise they'll always be in touch, only to cut all contact with you a few months after the divorce is final. Some of them will "take your side" and some won't. Your in-laws' behaviors stem from their own subconscious programming. They don't know all the facts pertaining to the breakdown of your marriage, but even if they did, their perceptions would still determine their behavior. That said, don't become prey of your ego's need to "set things straight" by giving your spouse's family a detailed recounting of what "really" happened. Stay in contact with these people because you love them and want them in your life. Any other reason is likely not aligned with your Highest Self.

Spiritual Organizations

This category includes any group of people who gather to share their spirituality, such as church groups. Whether or not you are religious, the *usually* uplifting and quiet environment in places of worship helps you connect with others and with God. I used the word *usually* because some religious organizations encourage low-energy emotions such as hatred and intolerance in the name of their ego-created image of God.

Make sure the church you select is aligned with what is truly divine: love. By physically being in one of these love-filled churches, you'll be aligning yourself with higher energies. Also, churchgoers generally tend to calibrate at higher levels of consciousness. Because high energies weaken and nullify low energies, your consciousness will be elevated by associating yourself with this group of people.

I used to stay at church after service, when the building was empty. I would sit in front of the altar and surrender all my feelings to God. Somehow, I would always bump into a minister or someone who just happened to be there at the right moment to offer a smile or a hug. My church visits lightened my heart and renewed my strength.

Connecting to Love:
The Ego's View

By definition, the ego is disconnected from love. First, the ego is absence of God, and God's essence is love. Second, the ego represents attachment, and where there's attachment, there's no room for real love. I'm not only talking about the love you receive from others, but also about self-love. Your ego is always looking for evidence that you are not worthy of love.

Your spouse leaving is one of the strongest forms of rejection you may experience from one of the people you cared about the most. Your ego will tell you this rejection is proof that something is wrong with you. You might repeat negative affirmations, such as:

- I'll never be able to love again.
- I'll never be able to find someone who loves me.
- Love always brings pain.
- I hate my spouse for leaving me.
- I must be a terrible wife/husband.

Fear is the opposite of love. God is love. Therefore, if you experience relentless fear, your connection to your Highest Self (God, love) is not clean.

Hatred is love going in the wrong direction. If you entertain hateful thoughts, you're moving away from God.

My self-esteem deeply suffered when my husband left. During the worst part of my journey, I felt removed from the ability to love and feel loved. I felt shame, which, according to David Hawkins' human consciousness scale, is the closest state to emotional death one can be. My self-rejection manifested itself in my pulling away from people who wanted to offer me their love and support. I didn't want anybody's love but my husband's. At the moment, I didn't see how powerful my egotistical attachment to him was.

Then my eyes opened, and I saw the truth.

You might be wondering how you can see the truth, too. The only way is by understanding the real meaning of love, which we will explore next.

Connecting to Love:
Your Highest Self's View

By connecting to love, you will also make a direct connection to God because God is love and love is God.

To feel connected to love, you must:

- Understand what love means.
- Understand the kinds of love.
- Love yourself.

- Be willing to connect to love by *being* love.

What does love mean? Love is not attraction or lust. Love is an entity that transcends all matters of the material world, including sex.

Love is not based on how well someone treats you and meets your needs. Love thrives on giving.

Love is not a fantasy, or an image of the way someone used to be or should become. Love is seeing people for who they really are in the present moment.

Love is not possession. Love is letting your loved ones follow their own paths, even if those paths lead them away from you.

Love is not controlling your loved ones' behavior. Love knows that since the people you love share the same universal consciousness, they will access their truth in time.

Love is not emotional attachment or codependency. Love is being complete without *needing* to have another person by your side.

Love is not compromising your core values for someone else's. Love brings up your Highest Self.

Love is not being married or in a romantic relationship. Love is intimate communion with another's soul.

Love is not rooted in your spouse. Love is rooted in yourself.

Love is not an emotion. Love is the essence of the Divine that manifests itself as unconditional acceptance of what is.

If your spouse claimed that the reason for his or her leaving was "falling out of love," lack of attraction, unmet personal needs, or that you're not good enough anymore, or that you didn't do what he or she demanded of you, then you can be sure that your spouse didn't know love.

In *The Way to Love,* Anthony de Mello explains that to experience love one needs to be able to say to the loved one, "I leave you free to be yourself: to think your thoughts, indulge your tastes, follow your inclinations, behave in ways that you decide are to your liking."⁵ You'll regain freedom when you're able to say this to your spouse with intention. Remember that regardless of your spouse's behavior, what matters is that you understand what love is so you are in position to connect with it.

What are the kinds of love? According to spiritual master Peter Deunov there are three kinds of love.[6]

- *Human love.* You may think of this kind of love as being at the junior or apprentice level. Human love is conditional, varies, and changes with time. This love mirrors the list you just read about what love is *not*. A person experiencing human love thinks, *If you're nice to me and do what I want, I'll love you. If you don't do what I want, I won't love you,* or *If you gain a lot of weight, I won't love you. If you get sick or are disfigured, I won't love you.* This is the love of the ego. "I fell out of love" or "I love you, but I'm not in love with you" are typical comments from someone who experiences human love.

- *Spiritual love.* This kind of love is closer to true love. Spiritual love sometimes varies, but never changes, like the love a parent has for a child. With spiritual love, forgiveness is almost effortless and compassion is always present. However, spiritual love allows room for being offended, so you might feel as though you would love the person less if they behaved in hurtful ways toward you.

- *Divine love.* Divine love never varies and never changes. This the true love that resides inside you, the love of God. With divine love you let go of your ego, and only love comes through you for yourself and everyone else, even people who've harmed you.

If you connect with your Highest Self, you'll experience divine love. Keep in mind that only intending to reach divine love will immediately raise your level of consciousness and lead you to happiness.

Who is your first love? You must love yourself and feel lovable before you're ready to give and receive love from others. When feelings of unworthiness creep in, remind yourself that you are a creation of God, and that by virtue of your own divinity, you're worthy of divine love. I encourage you to re-read the section in Chapter 2 in which you affirm, "I am love" instead of "I am worthless."

Are you willing to connect to love? To be willing means to have a burning desire to be love and to give love. To be willing means to be aware of your ego, so when you have unloving thoughts toward yourself or others, you immediately replace them with loving thoughts. To be willing means to be steadfast as you advance toward love and move away from negative energies.

I was able to let go of my sense of disconnection only when I understood what love truly meant, and recognized that my husband was his own person with his own mind, who was doing what he thought was best for himself. I put aside my feelings of worthlessness and was steadfast in my intention to love myself. I set myself on a path toward divine love, and by merely being on this path, I was able to love my husband without having to be married to him.

CHAPTER 7

Attachment to Detachment
Breaking the Chains

"He who would be serene and pure needs
but one thing, detachment."
—Meister Eckhart

Being attached to something or someone means believing that you can't be happy unless you *possess* that something or someone. Attachment is a common state of your ego, which always demands, always strives, and never arrives. Your ego demands to own the object or person it's attached to, and puts all its energy into its attachment. When your ego's demands aren't met, you sink down to low-energy vibrations, which prevent you from being your Highest Self. When your ego's demands are met, you experience a sense of temporary happiness that fades when you find a new attachment to strive for. You engage in a cycle that keeps you removed from the ability to experience freedom and happiness in the present moment. Attachments may be directed to something as mundane as having a cup of coffee in the morning, or to something as significant as your marriage.

Let's delve into the effects of being attached to your marriage. The strength of your attachment to a thing or a person will determine the intensity of your negative emotions when you lose the object of your attachment. The strength of your emotional attachment to your marriage might not have been evident to you until your spouse left, so you might be in a state of shock. You might spend most, if not all, waking hours analyzing your loss, wishing it hadn't happened, being angry about it, and fearing that you won't be able to recover. Your attachment might prevent you from eating or sleeping or simply functioning. While attachments will impair your connection with your Highest Self at any point in your life, emotional attachment to your marriage and your spouse has the potential to produce long-term spiritual damage.

You can view attachment as a form of fighting change. Newton's Third Law of Motion states, "For every action there is a reaction." The principle in this scientific law can be applied to human thought and behavior, which means that if you fight what you don't want, what you don't want will be returned to you. We will further explore this topic in the next chapter, where you will learn to nullify resistance with allowing.

In *Rediscovering Life*, author Anthony de Mello states: "The uprooting of sorrow means the uprooting, the dropping of attachments."[1] Visualize your attachments as chains that are preventing you from being truly free, and break out of those chains. Breaking free of the chains means you can still grieve your loss, but you won't be paralyzed by it.

It's important to note that detachment doesn't mean apathy (not caring). When you detach, you can access the positive energy required to make changes in your life because you aren't solely focused on what's missing. You still care, but you nevertheless continue to live a life of meaning.

In order to clean your connection with your Highest Self, eliminating all attachments is ideal. Here, we will concentrate on getting rid of common attachments associated with separation or divorce, such as an attachment to:

- The past.
- Your relationship.

- Your spouse.
- Your stuff.
- Your children.
- Your place in society.
- Your plans for the future.
- Fairness and being right.
- Your beliefs.
- Your current feelings about your relationship with your spouse.
- Your pain.

Attachment to the Past:
The Ego's View

Your attachment to the past might be directed in three different ways.

1. The happy times in your relationship.
2. The unhappy times in your relationship.
3. The way your spouse used to be.

The happy times in your relationship. No matter the length of your marriage, it's very likely you accumulated myriad positive memories that your subconscious mind linked to places, scents, music, activities—and even words. A lot of these stimuli will continue to be present in your life after your spouse leaves. At times you might feel as though you're being bombarded with reminders of life with your spouse. You might fantasize about moving to another city, or even to another country, where you will be free of these reminders. Thinking about how good things were might make you feel that you will never be happy again.

The unhappy times in your relationship. Day-to-day stimuli can awaken happy memories, and they can also bring up unpleasant ones. If you found out about your spouse's affair at a party, for example,

79

you might feel nauseated every time you drive by the location where the party took place, or every time you're offered food similar to that which you ate at the party.

Sometimes painful memory flashes will seem as though nothing has triggered them. You might be waiting in line at the grocery store, and all of a sudden the image of your spouse telling you he or she is moving out pops up. The thought comes from your subconscious mind, which is always working in the background, processing information you're not even aware of. These out-of-the-blue thoughts have the power to release low-energy feelings in a fraction of a second.

The way your spouse used to be. You might reject the reality of your spouse's desire to leave you, and may ask yourself over and over how he or she could possibly be doing this to you. You might tell yourself that this is a phase. You might tell people that you don't recognize your spouse anymore. You might wonder when or if your spouse will come back to his or her senses.

Psychologists would call what I just described "stages of shock and denial." I call them signs of *attachment*.

I experienced all three forms of attachment described above, and learned that they had one thing in common: the power to drag me in a direction contrary to where my life was supposed to be moving: forward.

These forms of attachment are like three strings of cans glued to the back of a bicycle. Every time you try to pedal forward, the cans clank against the road, capturing your full attention, and either making you stop or preventing you from enjoying the ride.

Besides triggering an onslaught of negative emotions, a common consequence of attachment to the past is the addictive behavior of overanalyzing.

The Trap of Overanalyzing

Preceding the word *analyzing* with *over* suggests that there's an excess of analyzing. While rigorously analyzing the minute details of complex statistical data might be helpful in science, overanalyzing something as subjective as a human relationship is not likely to yield useful results.

As an overanalyzer, you might use your waking and nonwaking hours (dreams) to accomplish one mission: to figure out why your marriage broke down. You might try to pinpoint the specific moment when your marriage started deteriorating, or the point at which it was definitely lost. You might try to remember the words you said at those moments, and berate yourself for the actions you took.

Overanalyzing tends to be a never-ending endeavor because one discovery triggers the need for more "discoveries." But let's say you eventually determine why your marriage ended, and let's assume your discovery is completely accurate and reliable.

Does it really matter?

The reason your relationship broke down doesn't matter to your marriage, because the fact is that your romantic union with your spouse is over, or is near its end already. However, the reason for the breakdown may matter to your *next* relationship if it prompts you to become a better partner than you used to be.

Even if positive change stems from this analysis, negative emotions such as anxiety, guilt, and shame may also arise. Analyzing tends to be a waste of time, and it's outright dangerous in high doses. If you continue analyzing what has already been analyzed, you'll remain firmly anchored to your problem and its causes.

I suggest that instead of analyzing, you go into quiet contemplation and determine how you can make changes that will help you better yourself, whether or not you intend to go into a new relationship in the future.

Attachment to the Past:
Your Highest Self's View

Regardless of what events in the past you direct your attachment to, it's still the past and therefore cannot be changed. Your past only has power when you decide to grant power to it. Only your present decisions can drive you toward happiness and fulfillment.

The way to detach from the past starts with awareness. Awareness is the common denominator in detachment from all things and all people. By being aware, you can stop ego-driven thoughts that might worsen your attachment.

Let's explore detachment from each of the three elements explored in the section above this one.

The happy times in your relationship. Remembering the good times can be beneficial because you'll understand that you didn't "waste" your life while married to your spouse. Regardless of the current situation, you had happy moments, learned lessons, and possibly welcomed children into your life. Listing all the positive things about your marriage might allow you to diminish your sense of regret, but as you do so, make sure that you don't develop a neurotic attachment to your idea that those were the *only* and *last* happy times in your life.

How do you detach from the nostalgia, and the sense that you will never be happy again? By being aware of these thoughts as soon as they appear, and replacing them with positive thoughts about the possibilities that your future holds. Is it possible that your future will be even happier than your past? Choose to think that this will be the case.

The unhappy times in your relationship. Even if you think your partner was at the most "fault" at the end of your marriage, you still played a role. Remembering the bad times can help you determine your role in the breakdown of the relationship so you can make positive changes in yourself. As you do so, however, beware of the overanalyzing trap. I suggest that you go into quiet contemplation and jot down ways to avoid repeating the thoughts and behaviors that produced your alignment with separation or divorce. At the end of each contemplative session, forgive yourself. Be as kind to yourself as you would be to an innocent young child who didn't know what he or she was doing. Extend unconditional love to yourself.

Below are additional strategies to detach from negative memories.

- *Meditate.* Surrender your negative memories to God and listen for a response. The response might arrive as an incredible sense of peace that washes over you, or even forgiveness. If no response comes to you, try again the next day. The answer will eventually be yours.
- *Reframe.* Realize that by letting your life be ruled by your bad memories, you're punishing yourself for something that can't be changed, and you're relinquishing control of your life to your past and to your spouse.
- *Spend time in nature.* Something as simple as a ten-minute walk in the woods will bring you closer to your Highest Self. Pay attention to the sounds, scents, and sights around you. Be in the moment. Let the negative memories pass through you, and visualize them being blown away by the wind.
- *Replace negative memories with positive ones.* If you currently associate a room in your home or a place outside the home with pain, then reprogram your subconscious mind by creating a positive experience in the same location.

The way your spouse used to be. This form of attachment is very much related to the human tendency to reject change. Picture a mother who cannot see her daughter as a grown woman and attempts to control that daughter's life. Do you see this mother-daughter relationship evolving as enriching and peaceful? In the same way, you need to realize that your spouse is not the person you married X years ago, but the person you see in front of you now. If we refer back to what real love it, we can see that loving others means accepting them for who they are, not for who they used to be.

Suggestions to see your spouse for who he or she really is include the following.

- If the conditions of your separation and the kind of relationship you have with your spouse allow for open communication, schedule "closing conversations" with him or her. Really listen to what your spouse has to say, and learn to see who he or she is at the present moment.
- List all the positive and negative traits you saw in your spouse when you were together. Then, list the positive and negative traits you've noticed in your spouse during your most recent interactions. Notice the similarities and differences between the two profiles. The differences might surprise you. Also, note the date you created the new profile to remind yourself that this profile will change again in the future.
- Realize that the only constant in your spouse is his or her divine nature. Your spouse is a creature of God regardless of his or her words or behavior. Choose to remain connected to this, the only real quality in your spouse.

Attachment to the Relationship: The Ego's View

This kind of attachment expresses itself as resistance to letting go of your married status. You might be afraid of being single again, or even worse, to be labeled "divorced."

Determine what being married means to you. Possible answers include:

- A sense of belonging in society.
- The idea of success, of having "done well."
- The sense of safety and protection in an uncertain world.

As you read this section of the chapter, you might resist the mere existence of this attachment, and say to yourself that you're not attached to being married, but rather, just devastated by the loss of your spouse. I initially thought the same thing, but as I became more aware of my thoughts and actions, and interacted with other people going through similar experiences, I realized that I had fallen prey to this kind of attachment.

Common behaviors that indicate attachment to the marriage include:

- Continuing to check the "married" box when filling out forms, covering the form so no one can see that you're not married, or checking "single" instead of "divorced."
- Flinching at the sound of the word *divorce*. Even my husband, who was the initiator of the process, was not able to say the D-word for over six months after he'd made his decision to leave our marriage.
- Avoiding people who knew you as a couple because they might ask about your spouse.
- Refusing to get together with divorced people because you're "not one of them."
- Thinking of yourself as "between marriages" just as laid off people think of themselves as "between jobs."
- Saying to yourself that because you got married by the church and haven't been divorced by it, you'll always remain married to your spouse, even if a legal divorce has been finalized.

Think of any other related behaviors or thoughts that you may be experiencing. Are you really letting go of your married status?

Attachment to the Relationship:
Your Highest Self's View

The process of detachment from being married is like going up a ladder with four rungs. The first of these rungs, as always, is *awareness*. The sense of belonging, success, and safety that being married provided you is a thought, and was created by the cultural programming you were subject to since you were born. Your relationship with anyone is a perception of the mind. The people you're in contact with, including your spouse, will have a different opinion of their relationship with you.

Picture someone from a television show that you watch every day. It could be the morning newscaster, or the host of a talk show. You probably feel as though you know this person. You might feel that you're friends—even more, best friends. You see this person every day, and she is always so smiley and welcoming. Then, one day you're grocery shopping and see this person. You rush to say hello, your cheeks warm with excitement, and the TV personality only gives you a polite smile. The person you thought was your best friend doesn't even know you.

The second rung to detach is *reframing*. If your spouse's feelings toward you remained the same (that is, your spouse wants to be apart from you), but you were given the power to make your spouse stay in the marriage, would you choose to do so? Even if your first reaction is to answer *yes*, I would expect that you would change your answer after more thought. You would realize that life by the side of someone who doesn't want to be with you cannot be pleasant at all. Also, reframe your damaged sense of self-worth. Your Highest Self isn't Mr. or Mrs. So-and-So. Remember that you are as magnificent as you have always been whether or not you're married.

The third rung is to *align yourself with your ultimate goal.* When a relationship prevents your connection with your Highest Self, that relationship is toxic, and you're better off walking away from it. Being attached to your relationship status is like being attached to a specific number on the scale and feeling that your day is ruined if you weigh a tenth of a pound more than you want to. Is this reasoning logical if your goal is to realize your Highest Self?

The fourth and final rung is to *modify the relationship with your spouse.* Since relationships only exist in your mind, you can make changes to your relationship with your spouse anytime you desire. You can choose to eliminate all the toxic portions of the relationship and only leave the elements based on love, respect, and kindness. Doing this might mean letting go of the marriage (if you're separated) or eliminating any form of contact with your spouse except when co-parenting.

You're at the end of the ladder of detachment. Picture yourself in a loving relationship with your spouse, and do what is necessary to achieve it.

Attachment to Your Spouse: The Ego's View

Your attachment might not only be directed to the way things used to be, such as to your marital status, but to the person with whom you used to share your life. This form of attachment, while accepted and even expected in our society, causes as much damage to your connection with your Highest Self as the other kinds of attachments.

You might have perceived your spouse as the only constant in your life. You counted on him or her to be there for you always. When your spouse left, you felt incomplete. You couldn't imagine your life without him or her. Even if your spouse hurt you deeply, it might be physically painful to not see or talk to your spouse every day. You might miss telling your spouse about your day, or telling your spouse about a funny joke you heard. You might miss snuggling next to him or her, feeling safe and warm.

If you're experiencing these emotions, you might be shutting down other people because no one else can replace the way your husband or your wife "made you feel." Your friends might try to cheer you up and spend time with you, your children might want to cuddle next to you, and your relatives might want to share meals with you, but in your mind spending time with other people just isn't the same. You might feel as though life without your spouse is only a series of activities with no meaning.

By being attached to your spouse, you're negating your own sense of self. You become dependent on your spouse's behavior, and you give yourself permission to be okay only if he or she decides to be with you. You decide to place the responsibility of your well-being on your spouse, and when you do so, it's as if you become your spouse's slave.

You are not free.

One of my favorite passages by author Anthony de Mello is: "They say that love is blind. Rubbish. There's nothing as clear-sighted as love. It's the most clear-sighted thing in the world. It's attachment that is blind."[2]

Attachment to Your Spouse: Your Highest Self's View

You can detach by redefining who you are, and by learning the difference between love and attachment.

Defining who you are. You must realize that by virtue of your own creation, you are divine. Every cell of yours is a miracle, and you have the power to access the wisdom of human consciousness. In *Three Magic Words*, Uell S. Andersen writes: "In all this world, there is not another you, nor has there ever been another you. Is it not ridiculous to attempt to mold yourself into a likeness of your fellows, to attempt to undo the work that God has done?"[3]

Andersen brings home the point of your magnificence. As a divine being, joy is at your disposal regardless of with whom you share your life. You don't need your spouse to exist, or even to have a happy existence. Think of the time in your life when you hadn't married your spouse yet. You were probably living your life without much trouble. Now isn't any different.

The difference between love and attachment. Earlier in this book, you read about replacing your sense of worthlessness with love. This is what attachment to your spouse means: You define yourself as worthless because he or she isn't by your side. Let's remember what love really means. As Anthony de Mello cleverly expresses in *Rediscovering Life,* "Love means, 'I'm perfectly happy without you, darling. It's all right.' It means, 'And I wish you good, and I leave you free. And when I get you, I'm delighted; and when I don't, I'm not miserable.'"[4]

Loving your spouse means letting your spouse make his or her own decisions, even if your ego tells you that you're right and that your spouse is making a mistake. Don't try to "fix" your spouse or to force him or her to "see the light." The best way to help your spouse is to give your spouse love. If you love your spouse, he or she will experience self-love, and this love will radiate back out to the world. Send your spouse away with love so your spouse can find his or her own path. Your main focus needs to be on your own journey, which has a clear destination: achievement of your Highest Self.

Attachment to Your Stuff:
The Ego's View

Your cultural programming will determine the strength and quality of this attachment. You might:

- Be so focused on the loss of your marriage and your spouse that you won't even care about your material possessions.
- Want to hang on to as much stuff as possible as a way to "compensate" for the pain you've experienced.
- Feel the need to keep as many things as possible because they represent the last string of connection to your married life.

One of the strongest attachments to the material is usually directed to the marital home. You might want to move out as soon as possible because being in the home is a constant reminder of your loss, in which case you'd be expressing your attachment to your negative association with the home. You might resist letting go of the home because in your mind, it represents a link to your marriage. Attachments cloud rational thinking, so you probably won't consider the financial feasibility of selling or keeping your home. If you want to keep your home, you might say to yourself and to others that you're doing it for the sake of the children so they have a stable environment. The truth is that you're acting out your own attachment.

Your attachment might also be directed to your furniture and decorations. You might be attached to the negative emotions associated with the furniture and dispose of it or even damage it to "get back" at your spouse. On the other hand, you might strive to preserve as much as possible and decorate your new residence in exactly the same way in which you designed your old home.

Finally, you might have to deal with attachment to larger assets and monetary income. The idea of halving everything (or being left with even less than half of the assets) might produce intense fear, and thoughts of shortage and lack might invade your mind.

Attachment to Your Stuff:
Your Highest Self's View

My main suggestion to detach from your stuff is reframing. *Needing* to keep more is like tying yourself to every item you supposedly require with a heavy rope. Needing material things might also launch you into a never-ending cycle of acquiring more stuff as a way to achieve a temporary sense of happiness. Shopping therapy, anyone?

Let's say your spouse, who never paid attention to the Afghan rug in your living room, says he or she wants it. All of a sudden, you feel the urge to possess this rug. After all, you picked it out at the store, and you have a better sense of decoration than your spouse. You use precious present moments to argue about who gets the rug. Eventually, after several stress-filled hours, you get to keep it. You expect happiness to come to you for "winning," but it doesn't. You say to yourself that maybe it wasn't the rug that you needed—it was the coffee table on *top* of the rug. You start to argue all over again. Do you think you'll find the happiness you're seeking if you continue "winning" and keep all the stuff? This example illustrates the vicious cycle and futility of attachment to the material.

Material things serve their purpose if you acquire them to meet your physical needs: shelter, warmth, transportation, and so on. Material goods are a problem only when you insist on hanging on to them because you feel that without them you'd be unhappy. When you detach, you might still want the Afghan rug, but if your spouse ends up taking it, you feel fine. You might actually feel even better than if you'd kept the rug because you gave something away, which is the behavior of your true nature. Remember that the God inside you only gives.

In short, regardless of the reasons for the dissolution of your marriage, be generous. When dividing assets, keep in mind both your own well-being and your spouse's well-being. This will not only result in peace for *you*, but in a much smoother process of separation.

Refer to Appendix A of this book, in which we explore the negotiation process. Make sure your list of goals also includes financial ones and the reason for those goals. When you're on the path to a clean connection with your Highest Self, the top of your list will read: "Peace." If you let peace guide you, you'll also achieve your financial goals.

Attachment to Time with Your Children: The Ego's View

Can you see yourself reflected in the behaviors below? If so, you're experiencing attachment to time with your kids:

- Not granting, or limiting, visitation rights as a way to punish your spouse for leaving the marriage. This is the you-made-your-bed-now-lie-in-it attitude.
- Not allowing the children to visit your spouse's new home with the pretense that the kids won't receive the care and comfort they're used to.
- Engaging in heated custody battles. Resisting shared custody "for the sake of the children," when there are no abuse or violence issues.
- Asking the children to report on any contact they've had with your spouse, and interrogating them about the details of their conversations.

This need to control your children's interactions with your spouse is a reflection of your fear of losing more people you love, and your resistance to acknowledging the end of your marriage.

By listening to the demands of your ego, you're closing your heart to the emotional needs that your children have with respect to being in contact with both of their parents. Also, your children are observing your behavior, which they might replicate in their future relationships. If your children's marriages fail, they're likely to behave in ego-driven ways and to blame their problems on their parents who just couldn't get along.

Attachment to Time with Your Children: Your Highest Self's View

You're probably wondering how you can possibly detach from your children. After all, they are *your* children. What bond could be stronger and more sacred?

Detaching doesn't mean not caring about your children. It means showing the love you have for them by doing what's in their best interest. Your ability to detach will allow you to see if your opinion about what's in their best interest is driven by love or by your ego.

With the exception of cases in which there's emotional or physical abuse, your children will benefit from the active presence of both parents during their growth. Sharing custody will be a huge change in your family dynamics, but as it usually happens with life changes, it will bring something positive to your and your children's lives. You might find yourself with time on your own to explore activities and hobbies you never had time for previously. Your children will witness how you and your spouse collaborate, and how you love them whether or not you live together. By sharing your time with your children, you're giving love, and giving is your true nature so you'll be in closer contact with your Highest Self.

As the poem by Kahlil Gibran says: "Your children are not your children. They are the sons and daughters of Life's longing for itself. They come through you but not from you and though they are with you they belong not to you."[5]

So let your kids be. Make your divorce a less traumatic transition by turning it into a learning experience about loving detachment.

Attachment to Your Place in Society: The Ego's View

You meet someone new, and sooner or later they ask, "Are you married?"

You and your family are known in the community as "The Smiths."

Your evening social routine consists of gatherings with other families or couples.

When people see you, they always ask about your spouse.

All of a sudden, everything changes.

You're not a couple anymore. You dread that people will ask you if you're married. You don't know what to say when people ask you how your spouse is. You don't know what group you fit in anymore, and you reject invitations from common friends. You feel as though you're facing another loss: that of your place in society. You imagine yourself rebuilding social connections on your own or with another partner, and the task seems daunting. Anxiety and fear keep you up at night.

I've been there. I remember saying to myself that it was best to be alone the rest of my life because making a whole new circle of friends seemed like an impossible task.

This form of attachment is akin to attachment to the relationship itself, which we've already explored.

The ego thinks that you *are* your reputation and what people think of you, so your change in social status threatens your ego's identity. To your ego, being married (happily or not) means that life is in order. Being divorced means that you've failed at life. Attempting to satisfy everyone's demands is a form of neurosis that can potentially determine everything you say and do, and which will severely impact your ability to connect with your Highest Self.

Attachment to Your Place in Society: Your Highest Self's View

Imagine that you're moving from a large home in the suburbs to a small apartment in New York City where pets aren't allowed. Even though you love your Irish setter, you offer him up for adoption. When the dog is adopted, will he care about what the other dogs on the block think? Will he think he's less of a dog for not being the Smiths' dog anymore?

Canines and humans might be different, but the essence of what we all are (creatures of God) is exactly the same. Regardless of the labels we've been given, we still are who we are. If you're not convinced of this truth, I ask you to imagine that you're part of a remote tribe in which there's no marriage or "married" labels. You grow up knowing that you might get together with someone of the opposite sex to reproduce, but you don't have any societal expectations from having had children with this person. If someone from the Western culture visited the tribe and told you, "You are not married," you would not feel like less of a person. You would probably just stare at the visitor with curiosity. You might even chuckle.

So reframe your idea of what being married means to your identity. If people judge you or stay away from you, that's their issue, not yours.

In addition to reframing, I suggest the following to detach from your social status.

- *Start your sentences with "I" instead of "We."* It's not *our* house, but *my* house. *We* didn't have a plumbing problem; *I* had a plumbing problem. These small changes will reprogram your new reality in your mind.
- *Make single friends with whom you can just be yourself without reference to the past.*
- *Face the subject of your fear.* Attend and enjoy social gatherings with old friends. If people ask you about your spouse, tell them the truth. If you're a woman who retook her maiden name, get new address labels with your favorite design.
- *Express yourself freely on whatever subject you're passionate about, even if you're being controversial.* At first, you might cringe if somebody makes a face, but with practice, you'll tame your ego's dependence on the good opinion of others.
- *Live your truth and love yourself.* Being left has nothing to do with your value as a child of God.

Attachment to Your Plans for the Future: The Ego's View

You'd already started searching for hotels for your next summer vacation with your spouse. It was your turn to celebrate the holidays with his family. You'd calculated how much your income and that of your spouse's would increase in the next ten years, and had created a savings plans based on the availability of these funds. You'd pictured yourself in your old age with your spouse by your side, sharing a cup of hot cocoa in front of the TV.

All those plans disappeared in a cloud of smoke.

It wasn't a mistake to make plans. Plans only become pernicious to your self-realization when your happiness depends on the attainment of what you'd planned.

Attachment to plans is attachment to living in the future. The ego avoids living in the present by either analyzing the past or worrying about the future. However, living in the present is the only true definition of living. By living in the past or in the future, you're not really living.

For example, even after my husband moved out of our house to "figure things out," I continued making plans for us as a couple, including outings and family gatherings. I didn't realize that I had become emotionally attached to my plans, so when they collapsed one by one, I sank deeper and deeper into despair.

Attachment to Your Plans for the Future: Your Highest Self's View

It's healthy to think of what you need to accomplish in order to follow your dreams, but it's not healthy to waste precious moments by collapsing into deep depression when something doesn't turn out the way you want.

How do you detach? There are two keys to detaching from your plans for the future with your spouse.

Key 1: Keep an open mind. As soon as you learn that something won't happen because you won't be with your spouse, look at the underlying "want" behind the plan. For example, your plan to go to your spouse's family reunion might have been prompted by your craving for a family connection. You could achieve this connection by visiting your extended family, or, if your relationship with your in-laws allows for it, by visiting them at a later date without your spouse. If your plans for the future are flexible, you'll be purchasing insurance against disappointment.

Key 2: Map out a new course. As plans with your spouse go awry, think of new and exciting possibilities for you alone. Take some time to think about what inspires you. Any activity that sends you into complete conscious awareness, during which time flies by without you even noticing is inspiring to you, so plan on including this activity in your schedule. Creative endeavors are guaranteed to lift you to higher levels of awareness because your imagination is closely tied to your subconscious mind, which is the mind of the Divine.

Attachment to Fairness and Being Right: The Ego's View

During all of your human interactions, your ego demands either a better outcome for you, or at the minimum, a 50/50 deal. The ego doesn't love for the sake of loving, or give for the sake of giving; the ego loves with the expectation of being loved back, and gives with the expectation of receiving. Your ego also expects to be rewarded when you follow the rules, and expects all the "bad people" to be punished. Bad things aren't supposed to happen to good people. This is why the god of the ego punishes the sinners and rewards the do-gooders.

But God does not know about punishments and rewards. Duality doesn't exist in God's mind. God only knows about love, and the only thing God can do is give.

Your ego's thirst for "fairness" might drive you to engage in actions and thoughts that will lower your level of awareness:

- Badmouthing your spouse.
- Dwelling in the loss of your marriage because you don't think you deserve something so awful happening to you.
- Laying the burden of the loss of your marriage on something external to yourself, such as your spouse's midlife crisis, illness, or a death in the family.

- Demanding revenge.
- Insisting on a contentious divorce.
- Continuing being unhappy until life is, by the ego's standards, fair again.
- Blaming God for the unfairness of your situation.
- Affirming that life is never fair to you, and sinking into hopelessness.

There are many other thoughts and behaviors I could list, but they're all rooted in your attachment to receiving when you give. Your attachment won't change your current life circumstances, and you'll waste precious moments striving for what is fair.

Attachment to Fairness and Being Right: Your Highest Self's View

The need for fairness is "an arbitrary vanity of positionality," as David Hawkins brilliantly expresses in *The Eye of the I*.[6] This means that when we say something is fair, we're extending a judgment based on our internal programming.

Letting go of judgment goes hand in hand with letting go of the need for life to be fair. I'm not suggesting that you become a doormat and allow your spouse to hurt you even more. What I'm suggesting is that you stop letting your judgment of your situation ruin your existence. In order to do so, you can practice the following strategies, which will automatically steer you back onto the path leading you to become your Highest Self.

Reframe the meaning of fairness. You decide what is fair or unfair, and your decision is based on the programming you were given as a child. Someone else might have a very different idea of what is fair, including your spouse, the lawyers, and the court judge. To a dictator, having sole authoritative power to decide the future of a country is fair. To your spouse, leaving the marriage to seek his or her own perceived happiness is fair. You can reframe your current situation by considering that what might be fair for you is to be out of a marriage in which you're not appreciated. What is fair for you might be to finally have time to be independent and explore what gives your life meaning. What is fair for you might be to finally take care of yourself.

Accept that life will not always fit your definition of fairness. Life *just is*. The people and situations around you *just are*. When you're tempted to be angry because your life isn't fair, remember that you're labeling your life using your own perceptions and beliefs. See the occurrences in your life as results of your past alignments, and remind yourself that you have the choice to align with energy patterns that result in happiness and fulfillment.

Remember the true nature of God. God is not up in the sky keeping tally of who's been naughty or nice, ready to punish the sinners and reward the do-gooders. God won't make your spouse suffer as much as you suffered. Your spouse might have a painful life if he or she chooses to be removed from his or her own Highest Self, but this is not for you to track or to decide. God is pure love. Connect to God by being love.

Place your attention on the gifts in your life. Remember your most precious currency: your energy. If you focus your energy on how unfair your life is, the universe will continue presenting you with opportunities to corroborate your belief. If you choose to invest your energy in what brings you joy and in the people who offer you love and support, you will be raised to higher levels of awareness; and the universe will provide you with joyful experiences and loving relationships.

Attachment to Your Beliefs: The Ego's View

A Course in Miracles teaches: "The world you see is an illusion of a world."[7] Beliefs are thoughts that you've repeated over and over in your mind. The repetition of a thought brings it into your subconscious mind, which is the universal mind that is always working in the background. Your subconscious mind can be seen as a recording device, while your conscious mind takes on the role of the message you record.

The relationship between the conscious and the subconscious minds can be portrayed as supervisor versus subordinate. Your conscious thoughts are constantly fed to your subconscious mind. When you wake up and think of yourself as a victim of abandonment, your subconscious mind hears: "I am a victim." When you go to bed and rehash how angry and sad you are for the problems in your marriage, your subconscious mind attaches the concept of yourself to hatred and hopelessness.

Your subconscious mind feeds your self-concept to your conscious mind, and this concept shapes your conscious thoughts and behaviors. Your subconscious mind creates in your experience what it believes to be true, whether or not you want it to materialize. When you're presented with a triggering event, your belief kicks in. The belief remains in your subconscious just like the knowledge of how to ride a bike.

Your ego is attached to your beliefs, because the ego always wants to be right and to win. To the ego, letting go of a belief is admitting defeat.

When you go through a separation or divorce, common repeated thoughts that might become beliefs in your mind are:

- "I'm not worthy."
- "There is no life after divorce."
- "This is just too hard to overcome."
- "There must be something wrong with me."
- "Everything bad happens to me."
- "I'll never be happy."
- "My children will be traumatized for life."
- "I'm too old to find love again."
- "I am alone."
- "I'll never be the same."

- "I'll never forgive."

When these thoughts become beliefs, and you live your life ruled by these beliefs, the universe will provide you with experiences that match them... whether you want it to, or not.

Attachment to Your Beliefs:
Your Highest Self's View

The first step to detach is to understand that:

- Beliefs are the result of repeated thoughts, which means that if you change your thoughts, you can change your beliefs.
- The ego is attached to your beliefs because it refuses to be wrong, but being wrong is a judgment, so this attachment is based on an illusion.
- Attachment to your defeating beliefs provides you with an excuse to be unhappy. After all, if you'll never be happy again, why even try to do anything that produces happiness?
- Attachment to your present beliefs—even if these beliefs are damaging—only seems safer and easier than attempting to think something different about yourself.

After you've understood the nature of your beliefs, you'll have to make a conscious choice to think differently.

Replace the previous self-defeating beliefs with these new ones.

- "I am a divine creation."
- "My life after divorce is brimming with possibilities."
- "I am overcoming the worst of this challenge."
- "I am becoming a better person."
- "I am learning (from my past mistakes) how to build a happy present and future."

- "I am grateful for everything I have, and I bring joy into my own life."
- "I am giving all my love to my children so they grow up to be empowered human beings."
- "I am full of energy and joy."
- "I am with God. The right people are coming into my life."
- "I am changing, but my changes are leading me down the path to self-realization."
- "I've already forgiven all who have hurt me in the past, including my spouse."

Notice that many of the new thoughts start with the words *I am,* so as to tap into the power of the Divine. Repeating these thoughts will transform them into your new beliefs. However, I do not suggest mindless repetition. Instead, *feel* the affirmation inside you, and visualize yourself as the possessor of that affirmation. If your affirmation is that you're changing for the better, imagine yourself already changed: being a good communicator, empathetic, self-assured, or possessing whatever quality you wish to improve in yourself. You must be able to visualize what it feels like to materialize your belief. The feeling that stems from these affirmations will be good, and when you feel good, you feel God.

Attachment to Your Current Feelings about Your Relationship with Your Spouse: The Ego's View

This form of attachment can be directed in two ways.

You think that your relationship with your spouse is forever damaged. Being attached to the thought that you and your spouse will never be in contact again because there has been too much hurt will block any possibility of a future friendship. If you have children, you might have a hard time co-parenting, which will not only impact your and your spouse's lives in a negative way, but also your children's lives.

You believe that in order to be happy again, you and your spouse must and will get back together in the future. If you've fallen prey to your desire to reconcile even after your spouse has clearly stated that he or she wants you out of his or her life, you run the risk of:

- Accepting demeaning or disrespectful behavior from your spouse.
- Moving away from your ultimate goal to connect to your Highest Self.
- Wasting present moments by living in the future, when you "hope" you and your spouse will be back together and you will finally be happy.
- Sinking to low-energy levels when there are new or clearer indicators that reconciliation will not occur.
- Damaging your relationship with your spouse even more by placing unrealistic demands on him or her.

Regardless of the way you choose to direct your attachment, your ego will insist on this attachment as an illusionary sign of strength. After all, the ego thinks that changing your mind is a sign of weakness.

Attachment to Your Current Feelings about Your Relationship with Your Spouse:
Your Highest Self's View

Detachment, as we've seen in previous situations, requires a hefty dose of awareness and actions that are aligned you with your Highest Self.

In this case, awareness starts by seeing that:

All your relationships are in your mind. Remember that a relationship is nothing more than a belief you have about a specific person. If you believe that you and your spouse do not and cannot have a positive relationship, then that's what you'll experience. Using the same logic, the relationship your spouse has with you is also in his or her mind, and this perception of the relationship might be very different from your perception.

As your life situation changes, your relationship with your spouse will change. How could be positive or productive to insist on a certain way of thinking when your situation has changed? In the words of Emerson: "A foolish consistency is the hobgoblin of little minds."[8] Give yourself permission to change your mind about the relationship. Remind yourself that changing your mind is not a sign of weakness, but a sign of true and complete awareness of your present reality.

Your happiness does not depend on the kind of relationship you have with your spouse. You have the sole power to decide when to be happy and to define whether your relationship with your spouse will be positive and enriching or negative and draining.

In addition to developing your sense of awareness, I suggest you try to:

Express your feelings to your spouse without expecting improvement or damage to the relationship. You might choose to write a letter (which you don't necessarily have to mail) or to engage in an honest conversation.

Ensure your mind is open to new relationships. This is especially important if you believe that you and your spouse might reconcile in the future. The truth is, there's no guarantee of reconciliation. By keeping your heart open to receiving love from someone else, you're allowing yourself to live your life to its maximum potential.

Engage in new activities and meet new people. Expanding your social circle will also expand your view of human relationships.

See your spouse as a creature of God, and as someone you're connected to even if you're not physically together. This perspective will allow for a more positive relationship while co-parenting or while establishing a friendship. At the same time, this way of looking at your relationship will allow you to cope if the reconciliation you wish for doesn't occur.

Attachment to Your Pain: The Ego's View

You might be attached to feeling depressed, angry, and hopeless. You might be attached to being the center of attention, to being the "poor you" who was left behind. It's easy to fall into the role of the fixer, and then, when the relationship can't be fixed, into the role of the victim. Maybe your routine is to wake up, feel sorry for yourself, tell anyone you see about the progress—or lack of progress—in your situation, badmouth your spouse to whoever is willing to listen, go through your workday distracted and unmotivated, and end your day by either calling a friend to complain about your situation or reading the latest marriage-saving or self-help divorce book. Your post-separation or divorce routine gives you pain, but it's familiar, so it feels safe.

After my husband and I separated, I noticed that my attachment to my pain had its roots in my desire to resist the situation, which is another element of the ego. I was afraid that if I stopped feeling pain and admitted to being "okay," then there wouldn't be any reason for my marriage to be saved. But if I remained in distress, God or somebody would intervene to make things better, and that would mean that my marriage wouldn't end. Deep inside, I knew this was neurotic thinking, but I still chose those thoughts. The reward of non-acceptance was too enticing.

Attachment to pain might bring about neurotic rewards, but it also brings about additional pain. When pain takes over your life, you usually find yourself sinking to even lower levels of energy, and continue attracting experiences that perpetuate the pain. For example, you might start having "accidents": You could, for instance, trip over the sidewalk while walking, drop a jar of tomato sauce, or let the dog run away. You might forget commitments and miss deadlines at work. This is what happens when you align with the role of a victim.

Pain prevents you from engaging in productive action. Attachment to pain prevents you from being happy.

Attachment to Your Pain: Your Highest Self's View

First of all, it's not wrong to feel temporary pain and sadness. What limits you and damages your connection to your Highest Self is your unwillingness to let go of the pain.

Once you've reached a clear and strong connection with God, pain will have no place in your heart, or if pain touches you, it will quickly leave you. However, if your connection isn't clean yet, you might experience extended periods of pain. These challenging times don't mean that you'll cling on to the pain for the rest of your life. Only *you* will decide when it's time for you and your pain to part ways.

How will you know that you're ready to make the conscious decision to be happy? Your intuition will tell you. Subtle, yet clear signs that you're ready to make the shift are:

- You feel excited about activities or spending time with people. You accept invitations to social gatherings.
- You find yourself labeling a day as "happy."
- When people ask you how you are, you don't ignore the question or answer, "Hanging in there." Instead, and without much thought, you answer, "I'm okay," or "I'm doing well."
- You start laughing again.
- You catch yourself making plans for the future (your *own* future, without your spouse).
- You stop thinking about your situation a few minutes a day, then a few hours a day, until a full day has gone by without a thought about it.

Here are three suggestions to help you detach from your pain.

- Realize that even if you feel miserable all day, every day, and even if you don't eat or sleep and are so sad that you want to end your life, no one with a magic wand will appear to make things better. However, your situation might worsen because you'll be attracting more painful experiences into your life.
- Practice a visualization exercise in which you step out of your body and observe yourself playing the role of a victim. What do you look and sound like? Would you want to spend time with yourself? This exercise will help you see the negative impact and futility of attachment to pain.
- Delay the pain. When you start having thoughts of pain and sadness, decide to postpone these thoughts and the accompanying feelings for 15 minutes, then 30 minutes, then an hour. Just like waiting to give in to a food craving, waiting to feel pain might eliminate the urge to feel it.

By breaking free of attachments, you will not only heal from the experience of separation or divorce, but will experience positive transformation in all aspects of your life.

CHAPTER 8

Resistance vs. Allowing Letting Go

"The flexible are preserved unbroken."
—Lao Tzu

Resistance is the third main component of the ego, and an obstacle for detachment. Let's explore how to dissolve resistance.

Resistance

The ego resists change, which is ironic, since the ego is the always changing, unreal part of you.

By resisting the current situation in your life, you're applying a force. By applying a force, a reactive force of the same magnitude will be exerted upon you. It's Newton's third law of motion, a scientific principle that can be applied to the realm of human emotion. So, if you resist being left behind, your spouse will want to leave you even more. If you resist being alone, more loneliness will come your way. Notice the parallels with the Law of Attraction. The universe reacts to the force you're applying to the different situations in your life by providing you with opportunities to continue experiencing those situations.

Denial is a form of resistance. I abhorred the word *denial* from the first moment I read it in a divorce book. According to the books and many online articles I read, I was supposed to go through the "denial" stage. I resisted the idea of being one more statistic experiencing the five stages of grief in the Kübler-Ross model.[1] I fought my supposed fate to be in denial, which strengthened my feelings of resistance. Looking back, I was denying being in denial. But regardless of the word you choose to describe resistance, the final effect is a slowdown of your progress in having a successful and joyful life. Resistance is a self-imposed hurdle that will prevent you from reaching your Highest Self.

Allowing

When you allow, you let changes happen. You let go of your attachments. You let life run its course. I can draw an analogy between resisting the end of a relationship and the portrayal of resisting cancer in *Dying to Be Me* by Anita Moorjani. Moorjani narrates how she fought cancer, desperately trying to find a cure for years, while her symptoms only worsened. It was only when her organs were shutting down and she was as physically weak as she could ever be without dying that she decided to let go. She allowed the cancer to do whatever it needed to do, even if this meant ending her life.

The result? She had a near-death experience in which she underwent a spiritual rebirth that translated into a physical rebirth. She woke up from her coma and was miraculously free of cancer in record time. Translating this experience into the end of your relationship, if you resist the breakdown of your marriage, you'll probably only make matters worse for you and for your spouse. If you let your spouse leave as he or she desires and send your spouse love in the process, you might end up with a restoration of you relationship. This relationship might not involve reconciliation, but open communication, respect, and the underlying love that you and your partner shared during your time together.

My fight against my marriage problems lasted nearly three years. I wanted to be in control. Even thinking about my marriage ending caused me to have severe stomach upset. I was in deep pain, and the ensuing days, weeks, and months passed by while I waited for my efforts finally to pan out.

I fought a solitary battle against divorce by reading books, going to individual and marriage counselors, and having relationship talks. Nothing seemed to work.

Then, one day, I said to God, "I did everything I could. Now it's in your hands." That's when an internal shift started to occur. And just as Anita Moorjani came back to life with full awareness, I also returned to my own Self with full understanding of who I was and what I wanted to get out of life. I trusted the divine wisdom within me.

How can you promote this shift within you?

The answer is in surrendering.

Surrendering

Surrendering is one of the cornerstones of the recovery movement. Summarized in a sentence: "Let go and let God." Summarized in a word: *Trust.*

Surrendering means to *know* that you are on the path you're meant to follow, and because of this, that all the pieces are falling into place to lead you *home*, where you belong. When you allow yourself to let go, your low-energy emotions dissolve in their own weakness, and your high-energy emotions remain strong and pure.

You can surrender by:

- *Being true to yourself.* To reach authenticity, all of your behaviors need to reflect your core values. Create a list of values that are true to you *now*, and when you're not sure whether to pursue an action or not, ask yourself how well this action matches these values. For example, eating a pint of

Rocky Road ice cream won't match your value of treasuring the magnificence of your body. Damaging your spouse's image through social media will not match your values of being love and being at peace.

- *Listening to your intuition.* Become quiet and wait for divine guidance. Once you've received that guidance, follow it. Remember that sometimes clear guidance will not appear as quickly as you desire. However, sitting in silence will allow you to regain peace, and a peaceful mind is closer to Spirit. Push aside excuses about being "too busy" to have a quiet moment. Time waiting at the doctor's office or at a traffic light is an opportunity to take a few deep breaths and regain peace.

- *Loving yourself.* Understand that you are a divine being, and treasure your magnificence. You are your first love, and you'll only be able to love others when you love yourself.

- *Being aware that everything in the universe is in divine order.* By letting go, you let universal consciousness take over, and lead you to where you're meant to go and to meet the people you're meant to meet. If you doubt whether your separation or divorce was supposed to happen, remind yourself that the proof it was supposed to happen is that it happened.

- *Trusting the wisdom of the universe regardless of your current circumstances.* You might be tempted to return to an attitude of resistance if the peace or the love you expect to materialize in your life isn't apparent. You might want to "will" quick emotional healing, and become frustrated when time passes and you still feel lousy. But you must remember that what you desire might turn into form in ways you never expected, and at a time that might not match your own timeline. The reason is beyond your comprehension; it's the power of the universal mind at work.

- *Being aware of the now instead of regretting the past or fearing the future.* By being in the now, you are establishing direct connection with your Highest Self, who can only exist in the now.

Remain steadfast in your resolve to surrender, and be gentle with yourself if, when you finally thought you had let go, resistance comes back with a vengeance. I had several ups and downs after my divorce, and I might still have several more to come, but these days most of my life is about allowing and not about resistance, and this is what matters. Consider the surrendering process as an 80/20 diet. If you *trust* at least 80 percent of the time, you'll remain on the path to achieving your Highest Self.

CHAPTER 9

Blaming vs. Taking Ownership
Reclaiming Your Power

"The search for a scapegoat is the easiest
of all hunting expeditions."
—Dwight D. Eisenhower

The last core aspect of the ego is to blame external circumstances for your unhappiness. Your ego will drive you to blame your spouse for every negative experience and emotion you encounter.

You're depressed because of your separation or divorce.

You forgot to pay a bill because you are stressed out, and you're stressed out because of your separation or divorce.

You can't sleep because you are anxious, and you're anxious because of your separation or divorce.

You're always sick because you don't take care of yourself, and you don't take care of yourself because of your separation or divorce.

I could fill dozens of pages with situations that you could blame on your marriage troubles. However, blaming is the ego's way to reaffirm its separation from everything and everyone, to remain attached to its current feelings and situations, and to resist change and positive action.

The only way to eliminate blame is to assume ownership for your marriage situation, even if you thought you did everything right and this "just happened" to you. The truth is your separation or divorce wouldn't have happened if you had not been aligned with it. Somehow, your actions or thoughts placed your relationship in a position to collapse. These actions could have been as evident as selecting someone who didn't share your commitment to marriage or as subtle as taking your spouse for granted and not appreciating his or her loving gestures for days, months, and years. Your thoughts could have been as evident as believing that you didn't deserve to have a happy relationship or as subtle as focusing on your flaws every time you looked in the mirror. Your behavior could have been as evident as avoiding physical closeness with your spouse or as subtle as avoiding deep conversations with your spouse for the fear of being ridiculed or rejected.

Maybe you pushed away your spouse for years without even realizing it.

Maybe you rejected yourself for years until your spouse rejected you as well.

Maybe you were waiting for your spouse to change to accept him or her.

Maybe you accepted your spouse's behavior even when you were being disrespected.

Maybe you chose to focus on what was missing in your spouse, so the universe magnified what was missing.

Maybe you didn't trust your spouse, and behaved in ways that created distrust in him or her.

Maybe you decided to stay in a relationship you knew was toxic.

Maybe your expectations of the relationship made it toxic.

Your situation is unique, so I suggest you take a sober look at yourself and contemplate, "What was my role in the breakdown of my marriage? How did I contribute to what happened?" The answer might not be evident. If it isn't, let some time go by before asking these questions again or you might fall for the trap of overanalyzing. In meditation, the answer will eventually come to you, and when it does, you'll be in a position to change.

Remember, you cannot control a situation over which you have no control. By owning the situation, you are in control and have the power to change it.

You might be saying to yourself that you cannot control your spouse leaving you, which is true, but you can control the impact this event has in your life and how you'll learn, and hence grow, from the situation.

If you refuse to take ownership of what occurs in your life, your ego will continue ruling your actions, so you're likely to repeat your failed relationship story with someone else. Once you take ownership and change, you'll be stepping onto the firm grounds that lead to self-realization and connection to your Highest Self.

PART THREE

Tools for the Journey

In Part One of this book, we explored the map of human consciousness and learned how higher, faster-vibrating energies are aligned with the Divine, while lower, slower-vibrating energies are linked to negative emotions. You learned how to raise the energy vibrations of your thoughts and how the Law of Attraction applies to your situation.

In Part Two, we explored ways to tame the four facets of ego: separation by connecting, attachment by detaching, resistance by allowing, and blaming by taking ownership of the situation.

In Part Three, I'll introduce you to five powerful tools that will help you journey through your separation or divorce and turn it into a learning experience. These are:

- Imagination.
- Approach to learning.
- Open mind.
- Patience.
- Meditation.

I invite you to see the process of healing and reaching your Highest Self as the most valuable and sacred "video game" you'll ever play, and the five tools you'll learn are like special wands that will allow you to reach the highest level of the game.

CHAPTER 10

Your Imagination
The Power of Your Subconscious Mind

"Everything you can imagine is real."
—Pablo Picasso

Imagination is where reality is born. A powerful thinker such as Einstein declared that imagination is more important that knowledge.[1] Your imagination is one of the most powerful tools available to you during separation and divorce, because your imagination will allow you to see the possibilities for your present and future. Imagination is a tool for manifestation.

There are two components of your imagination: your thoughts and your feelings. You must understand the potential power of both to materialize a happy life without your partner.

The Power of Thought:
Your Conscious and Subconscious Minds

You're aware that your thoughts can be sources of joy or pain. Your thoughts drive your feelings and your behaviors, so by controlling your thoughts, you'll have a firm grip on the direction of your life.

Let's prove that it's possible to control your thoughts. Try a simple exercise.

- Think of a lime-green giraffe.
- Make bright orange spots appear on its skin.
- Make the giraffe sprout wings and fly.

I have no doubt you were able to accomplish this exercise without effort. How did you do it? You *just did it*. You have tested a universal truth: You are in control of your thoughts, and controlling these thoughts is a choice you can make any time you want.

You might be thinking that you cannot control *all* of your thoughts. After all, you're still haunted by the thought of your marriage situation when you're in the middle of a work meeting or by the thought about your uncertain financial future when you're picking up your children from school. You can't really help it.

These seemingly uncontrollable thoughts are driven by your subconscious mind. Your subconscious mind has been programmed from the moment of your birth with millions sources of information and sensorial perceptions. Your subconscious mind is in tune with human consciousness, and is the vehicle through which the Law of Attraction works in both your present and future. Therefore, controlling those thoughts that arise from the subconscious is the key to manifesting your desires.

Is this really possible?

It is. Just as your subconscious mind was programmed to produce the negative thoughts you're having now, it can be reprogrammed to have thoughts aligned with your Highest Self.

Reprogramming your subconscious mind requires:

- Shifting thoughts and behaviors upon awakening.
- Being aware of subconscious thoughts throughout the day.
- Shifting thoughts and behaviors before going to sleep.

Note that I'm not suggesting you list all the negative thoughts in your subconscious mind and "fight them." Light (positive energy) overrides darkness (negative energy). This means that reprogramming only requires bringing the high-energy thoughts to your mind without focusing on the low-energy thoughts. The low-energy thoughts will naturally dissolve.

The process of reprogramming requires willingness and discipline. We can find a good analogy when we consider what it's like to start an exercise program; at the beginning, you have to put more effort into it, and will probably experience delayed-onset muscle soreness. But as you become more fit, exercise will become easier and eventually second nature. You'll wake up ready to exercise. In the same way, higher awareness will become second nature to you when most of the thoughts you feed to your subconscious mind are high-energy thoughts.

Let's review each element of the reprogramming process.

Shifting thoughts and behaviors upon awakening. The moments immediately after you wake up set the tone for the rest of the day. There might be a period after your spouse leaves the marriage in which you'll be mourning your loss. During my separation, I would open my eyes each day and start crying. If this happens to you, let the tears come, but don't become attached to those tears.

Even if you're not ready to stop mourning, make it a habit to start your day by giving thanks to God for being alive. Visualize all the blessings in your life: family, friends, a bed to sleep in, food, and even the little rest you managed to have. Then, picture yourself having positive, joyful interactions with those around you. This is one of Louise Hay's most notable suggestions for a fulfilled life: to use daily affirmations upon awakening that align you with high-energy vibrations.

Being aware of subconscious thoughts throughout the day. Your senses are bombarded with stimuli. These stimuli might not be detected by your conscious mind, but they'll be processed by your subconscious. This is why seemingly random thoughts about your past or about your uncertain future can strike without warning; you're responding to your subconscious programming.

Do not fear these thoughts. Let them come to you as they may, but be aware of them. When you're conscious of a thought that might trigger negative emotions, either replace it with a positive affirmation or approach it from a different perspective.

Let's say you're in the cereal aisle at the grocery store. All of a sudden, you picture you and your spouse sharing a bowl of muesli at the kitchen table. The thought of never sharing that bowl of muesli again follows. Before a wave of sadness and hopelessness hits you, become aware that you're letting the past rule the present, and choose to see the breakfast memory as proof that the time you shared with your spouse wasn't a waste. You have proof that there were happy moments in your marriage, and those moments are yours to keep. Then, affirm to yourself, "I am grateful for my past moments with my spouse, and I am happy now."

Shifting thoughts and behaviors before going to sleep. Right before you go to bed, when there are no items on your to-do list to tackle or TV to muffle the internal chatter in your head, the thoughts of your loss tend to resurface with renewed energy. You think about what you could have done differently, or feel angry at having a failed marriage, or imagine a terrible future alone. You find you're unable to sleep or fall into a restless sleep with these negative thoughts in mind. If you do this, you'll be programming your subconscious mind with the information about a life that you don't want, even if your goal is to be joyous and fulfilled.

The subconscious mind cannot tell the difference between what you want and what you don't want, so if you think about what you don't want or what you don't like immediately before you go to sleep, your subconscious mind will be soaking up this information during the next eight hours. When you awaken, your subconscious mind will provide you with thoughts and experiences that match its negative programming.

To reprogram your subconscious mind, you may do one or more of the following the moments before you go to sleep:

- Make a conscious connection with your Highest Self through meditation or prayer.
- Give thanks for the positive events of the day and for the people in your life who care about you.
- Focus on the possibility of your finding joy, love, and peace. Even if you feel so wounded that the possibility of being happy again seems small, focus on that possibility, because at least this way you'll be directed to the path to happiness.
- Visualize yourself healing, and *feel* what it feels like to be healed. (We'll explore how to use visualization in this way in the next section.)

After experiencing the power you can exert on your thoughts, you'll know that you can control your beliefs, because beliefs are no more than repeated thoughts. Beliefs are to the subconscious mind what apps are to cellphones. What are your current beliefs? Are these beliefs serving you? If not, determine what thoughts are producing the negative beliefs and start the reprogramming process.

The Power of Feeling:
Assuming the Feeling of the Wish Fulfilled

Feelings are the second component of your imagination. You already know that you have the power to control your thoughts. You also know that thoughts trigger emotions and feelings. Therefore, you have the power to control your feelings.

The ability to control your feelings not only allows you to remain at high levels of awareness; controlling your feelings leads to the materialization of your desires. How is this possible? It all centers on the divine power of the subconscious mind, and your ability to tap into this power if you assume the feeling of the wish fulfilled. As Neville Goddard expresses in *The Power of Awareness,* "First, visualize the picture in your consciousness. Then feel yourself to be in that state as though it actually formed your surrounding world. By your imagination that which was a mere mental image is changed into a seemingly solid reality."[2]

The key is to not simply visualize your desire, which would just be daydreaming, but feeling what it feels like to attain what you desire. Once you have assumed this feeling, you'll have *experienced in your body* what it feels like to achieve your wishes. This is so critical because only by directly experiencing something can your subconscious mind adopt it as your reality.

In *The "I Am" Discourses,* Saint Germain asserts, "Nothing ever really means anything to anyone until he uses it."[3] This means that receiving information is the first step in transformation, but you won't be transformed until you internalize this knowledge. David Hawkins likewise states in *The Eye of the I,* "To know all about China doesn't make one Chinese."[4] Let's apply this insight to your situation.

Someone could tell you how there will be a time in which your grief will leave, and you'll be able to open your heart to romantic love again. If you only listen to these words without feeling what it would be like to be at peace and in love, you'll only be fantasizing, and will return to negative energies soon after your attention returns to your current situation. However, if you experience in your body the peace and the excitement of new romantic love, these emotions will become real for you, and your subconscious mind will connect with situations and experiences that will allow you to materialize your desires. Remember, to *know about* something is very different than *to know* something because you have lived it.

With God, all things are possible, which leaves nothing out. *Anything* you want to achieve is within your grasp, even overcoming the pain of separation or divorce and forgiving your spouse.

Special considerations when applying the divine tool of visualization are that:

- *Your desire must be aligned with Spirit.* If what you want to accomplish involves revenge against your spouse, you'll be aligning yourself with low energy levels during your visualization, and more opportunities to seek revenge will appear in your life. If you were left for another person, anger and hatred might move you to wish harm to the "other woman" or the "other man." By doing this, you will only be attracting harmful circumstances into your life.

- *In order to reprogram your subconscious mind by assuming the feeling of the wish fulfilled, you must be in a state of peace and true connection with God.* If you're tormented by sadness, hatred, anger, or anxiety, you won't be able to tap into the power of manifestation. This is why I suggest preceding your visualization exercises with meditation.

- *You must be clear about what you want, and visualize it in great detail in your mind.* "Feeling happier" is not clear. "Making one new, long-lasting friendship in my kickboxing class" is clear.

- *Your desire must feel natural to you.* Positive affirmations without positive expectations to back them up won't yield positive results. This means that if being happy seems impossible to you right now, you need to gradually elevate yourself to a state of happiness. If you are experiencing hopelessness and deep anguish, start by moving up to a state of emotional neutrality. Only you know the pace at which your subconscious mind can be reprogrammed.

- *You need patience.* In a universe in which there are no accidents, events happen in divine order. If you become anxious about the manifestation of your desire, you'll be bringing a low-energy field to the equation, and will prevent your desire from manifesting. It might be difficult for you to be patient when you feel that life has treated you so poorly. You probably want your everyday existence to be better. Now! And it can be better now if you choose to focus on the small steps that you're taking toward truth and freedom.

A day without crying is a triumph. An hour without thinking about your situation, another triumph. Celebrate the little successes as you travel through the tunnel of separation or divorce and into the light of your new life.

- *You must focus on your own life.* Trying to manifest anything for other people usually has an egotistical origin, so you won't be able to truly connect with God. I used to visualize my husband "coming to his senses" or "seeing the light." I didn't realize that my underlying motive was to satisfy my emotional attachment to him. Needless to say, this visualization became only a useless fantasy in my head.

Tying Thoughts and Feelings in with Behaviors

You're aware that you have the power to control your thoughts and your feelings. Now you can tie your high-energy thoughts and feelings in with behaviors that will reinforce those new thoughts and feelings. What this means is that your reprogramming will drive you to act in ways that will continue to raise your levels of awareness. Examples of the ways in which your subconscious mind's programming translates into the manifestation of your desires are as follows.

- *You visualize and feel unconditional love coming to you and emanating from you.* Your subconscious programming says you are love and worthy of unconditional love. One day you go to your local library and notice a post on the community board about a networking event, and for no apparent reason you feel urged to attend this event. During the event, you meet a person living at high levels of awareness with whom you immediately connect. As time goes by, this person becomes a provider and recipient of unconditional love.
- *You think of yourself as peaceful and free of anxiety.* You visualize and feel what it's like not to be tormented by your past and to look forward to the future. One morning, you pick up the newspaper, and notice an announcement for a new meditation class in your area. You decide to give the class a try, and become skilled at meditation. Your ability to achieve

peace brings enlightenment in your life, and your current situation no longer acts as a source of anxiety.

- *You think of your body as a divine creation.* You visualize yourself radiant and full of health, shedding old poor habits and regaining the vitality you had before your marital problems started. One day you wake up early and decide to go for a run instead of sleeping in. You love the experience, and running becomes a new passion for you. As your training continues, your body becomes fit and strong and vibrant just as you imagined it.

When your thoughts and feelings are aligned with your Highest Self, positive transformation happens. There's no way to stop this change because the power of the Divine is within it. You'll be able to see what was once shrouded behind the cloud of the ego. Furthermore, the situations, people, and things required to materialize your desires will come into your life exactly at the time you need them. This is what Carl Jung called *synchronicity,* a phenomenon that we will explore in further detail in Chapter 15.

CHAPTER 11

The Way to Learn
You Can Be a Step Ahead

"The intuitive mind is a sacred gift and the rational mind is a faithful servant. We have created a society that honors the servant and has forgotten the gift."
—Albert Einstein

Any challenge presents opportunities to learn, but bigger challenges usually provide more significant opportunities for growth. This means that the challenge of separation or divorce in your life might have the largest potential for learning and growth in your entire existence. However, learning can happen in different ways, each with various amounts of psychological and spiritual pain. My goal is to help you choose the most efficient way to learn while minimizing that pain.

According to Wayne Dyer, there are three ways to learn in life.

- Learning by looking back (LL)
- Learning in the now (LIN)
- Learning by stepping ahead of a problem (LS)

These three means of introspection will eventually result in personal growth, but they differ in their timing and the level of pain you'll experience. The illustration below shows the differences between the three approaches:

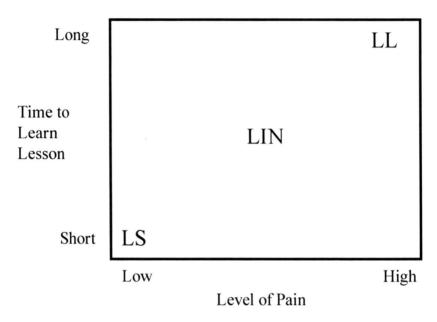

Learning by Looking Back

Learning by looking back is the method most of us use throughout our lives. We live through a tragedy or a difficulty, and months or years after it's over, we understand why we had to go through the challenge. Usually we're able to draw lessons out of the situation. If we apply these lessons, we avoid making the same mistakes or attracting the same situation. If we don't apply the lessons, life usually presents us with a "retest" until we can learn and change. How many times have people married the same person in a different body or accepted the same meaningless, stressful job with a different company? Most of us eventually pass the "test" and don't have to suffer going through the same unpleasant situation over and over again.

The problem with this method is that we experience a lot of pain for extended periods of time, and by the time we learn our lesson, we have wasted precious present moments.

When your marriage ends, you might spend years blaming your spouse for your unhappiness. If this is the case, you're likely to bring your negative energy and behaviors to your next relationship, which is likely to fail. Ten years might go by until one day you realize the role you played in the breakdown of your marriage and in your perceived sense of happiness. This is not the easiest way to learn or to grow. After all, we only have a few ten-year periods to learn before it's time to leave this physical realm.

Let's illustrate how this learning method would apply to three common situations brought about by separation and divorce.

1. *Your teenage daughter is suspended from school.* You have a talk with her, and learn that she skipped school several times. You ground your daughter for the rest of the school year, and wonder how she could behave in such an inconsiderate way when she sees you suffering because of your marriage breakdown. As months go by, you realize that your daughter acted the way she did as a reaction to the negative environment in your home after your spouse moved out. You pinpoint the role you played in your daughter's behavior and change your ways. You and your daughter start having positive conversations that eventually lead to a healed parent-child relationship.

2. *Your spouse files for contested divorce and hires a shark-like lawyer.* You hire another shark, and not only spend thousands of dollars on attorney's fees but also have a traumatic experience in court. The relationship with your spouse is shattered, and your ability to co-parent effectively is impaired. Years later, you realize how the lack of communication between you and your spouse resulted in his or her desire to go to court, and you learn to be more open and empathetic in your future relationships.

3. *You're laid off apparently for no reason.* Losing your job and your marriage simultaneously bring incredible stress. You live your life thinking you're the unluckiest person alive

until years later you look back and realize how your negative emotions compromised your job performance, and how you would have been able to save your job if you had spoken with your manager about your situation. You have a spiritual awakening, and start to appreciate the blessings in your life, including your current employment.

As you can see, this way of learning results in distress that may persist for extended periods of time.

Learning in the Now

Learning in the now means to elevate your level of awareness so you can identify the lessons embedded in what is happening to you *now.* You take a step back, witness your experience, and discern the lessons presented to you. You have immediate power to apply the lessons and effect the change needed in your life. When you apply the lessons, you're not likely to experience the same painful situations again.

How could you apply this learning method to the three common situations explained before?

1. *You have thoughts of anger toward your spouse, so you start behaving in angry ways toward others, including your teenage daughter.* You receive a call from your daughter's school to say that she skipped school and will be suspended if she does it again. Your awareness allows you to immediately recognize the impact your behavior has on your child. Before the damage to your daughter worsens, you shift your way of thinking and your behavior, and have a loving talk with your daughter. Your daughter responds to the talk and to the positive changes she perceives in you, and stops skipping school.

2. *You think you'll be able to come to a peaceful financial and custody agreement with your spouse, but suddenly, all communication stops and then you receive a letter from the court with a trial date.* Your spouse wants a contentious divorce. Instead of wallowing in your "bad luck," you spend time in meditation and reflect on what you need to do. You prepare yourself as well as possible and research the options available to you. During the trial, you're able to step away from the situation and manage your thoughts of anger and revenge. You remain calm and composed as you face the judge and your spouse. You have a relatively short trial process and end up with a settlement that might not be exactly what you wanted, but is acceptable. After a period of healing has passed, you and your spouse can co-parent effectively.

3. *You have constant thoughts of anger that make it difficult to concentrate at work.* When you miss an important deadline that sends the whole office into a frenzied state, you realize the impact of your emotions on your performance. You assume the role of a witness to your negative thoughts, and replace blame and revenge with quiet contemplation. You remind yourself of the role you played in the breakdown of your marriage, take ownership for your current situation, and feel empowered to excel at work the next day. It takes a while to regain trust from your manager, but you eventually achieve it. You feel good about your own behavior and continue on your path to a clean connection with your Highest Self.

Although this is a much better way to learn than learning by looking back, you'll still have to go through the challenge and experience pain for growth to occur.

Learning by Stepping Ahead of a Problem

Learning by stepping ahead of a problem is pure higher consciousness. With this method, you follow your intuition (which is God speaking to you) to prevent the situation from happening in the first place, thus avoiding pain altogether. You remain in your highest energy field, and your connection with your Highest Self is clean and solid. You have no negative emotions clouding your thoughts, and if they appear, you're able to nullify them immediately. You tap into divine power.

Let's now see how the three situations we studied before unfold when you learn by stepping ahead of them.

1. *While you're spending time with your teenage daughter, a thought about a past hurt comes to you.* You start feeling a twinge of anger, but before the anger gets hold of you, you catch yourself. You remind yourself that this anger comes from being attached to the past, and that in order to truly enjoy life, you must live in the present moment. You ask your daughter to join you for dinner at her favorite restaurant, and afterward you both go to a funny movie. You hug your daughter and tell her that you and your spouse love her regardless of the separation or divorce. The thought of skipping school doesn't even cross your daughter's mind.

2. *During your interactions with your spouse, you notice that your spouse has become withdrawn and has that special look on his or her face that tells you something is bothering him or her.* You follow your intuition and ask if everything is okay, and state that you want to collaborate to remain at peace. Your spouse admits the current asset distribution doesn't seem fair, and that he or she wonders if the only solution is to go to court. You find a divorce mediator who is aligned with your goal to remain at peace. You and your spouse stay out of court during the entire divorce process, and you're satisfied with the

final agreement. You work as a team to raise your children in the most positive environment possible.

3. *You're in the middle of creating a spreadsheet at work, but find it difficult to concentrate because your mind is focused on the divorce process.* Anger starts bubbling inside you. Instead of continuing to waste your time staring at the spreadsheet, you go for a quiet walk and reach out to God. You let the angry feelings come through as they may, and trust that they'll eventually dissolve in their own weakness. Once you finish the walk, you acknowledge that your angry feelings might stay with you for a while longer, so you explain the situation to your manager, and request the rest of the day off to recharge. Your manager, who went through a divorce herself, empathizes with you. You spend the next few hours enjoying nature, and the next day, you feel like going to work again. You meet all project deadlines and your performance is as good as always.

Stepping ahead of the problem is the most efficient and least painful way to learn, but requires a clean connection with your Highest Self. Be kind and patient with yourself if you slip and let your ego drive your thoughts and actions. Your intuition is and will always be there, waiting for you to tap into it.

You know your spouse better than anyone, and this knowledge is a special aid to your intuition. Use what you know about your spouse to get through the process of separation and divorce as peacefully and quickly as possible. Continue using your intuition when you meet new potential romantic partners. Trust that your next relationship will be full of spiritual love instead of conditional, egotistical love.

Finally, remember that learning never ends. You might continue drawing lessons out of your separation or divorce even years in the future. As James Twyman states in *The Moses Code,* "Just because you've learned something, it doesn't mean the lesson is over."[1]

CHAPTER 12

An Open Mind
Your Key to Beating Uncertainty

"You'll miss the best things if you keep your eyes shut."
—Dr. Seuss

We've outlined how to control your thoughts and emotions, and how to more effectively learn during this time in your life. The next tool you'll need to continue the healing process is to have an open mind. Having an open mind goes hand in hand with a sense of detachment. When you're detached, you allow the universe to pour out its abundance upon you. As Albert Einstein stated, "In the middle of every difficulty lies opportunity."[1]

Opening your mind refers to being open in all areas of your life, but we'll focus on the four areas relevant to this time of transition. Have a mind open to:

Your spouse's opinions. During and after your separation, really listen to your partner. What your spouse says might sound irrational to you, but keeping your mind open to it will help you see your spouse for the essence of who he or she is. Being open is the true foundation of love. It might seem senseless to learn how to love someone who's leaving you, but only by truly loving this person, will you be able to let go.

Sometimes listening to your spouse will be extremely challenging. Be aware that your need to "drill sense" into your spouse is the result of the judging and controlling behavior of your ego. Let your spouse's words flow through you. Imagine yourself in his or her situation, believing that leaving the marriage will provide the happiness your spouse is seeking, but also dealing with guilt, anger, and fear at facing his or her own uncertain future. Your empathy might release a new wave of understanding and compassion in your heart.

My husband's reasons for leaving the marriage seemed to change every month. I learned to see him as an innocent being trying to find his path, and sent him love so he would eventually reach the clarity he was seeking. My role wasn't that of a teacher or proselytizer, but of a provider of love.

New experiences. It might seem safer to continue doing the same things you once did with your spouse, but deviating from your old routine might prove to you that life isn't ending because of your separation or divorce. Open up to experiencing a new set of environments and activities. If you don't like adventure races, try paddleboarding. If paddleboarding isn't your thing, take a yoga class. Keep testing and tasting what life has to offer.

How do you decide what to try first? Ask yourself what makes you be so consciously aware of the present moment that time seems to fly by, and seek related activities. Being in this state called *the zone* will raise your level of awareness. By doing what brings you to high energy levels, you'll meet people who are also at high levels of awareness.

I encourage you to keep tally of all the new things you try. This list will be a reminder of all the wonder that life offers, and will open your mind to even more possibilities.

Uncertainty. You might have experienced several degrees of fear, from a subtle hint of apprehension that goes with you wherever you go, to the paralyzing fear we explored in the first part of this book. Your fear is often rooted in thoughts about a seemingly uncertain future. When you learn to welcome uncertainty, you open the door to unexpected, yet beneficial experiences. A mind open to all kinds of possibilities is also more *aware* of opportunities that otherwise would have gone unnoticed. In short, you'll become "lucky."

Remind yourself that the only changeless element in your life is your connection to God. Trust that your divine nature will guide you to the right people and the right opportunities. When you trust, you have faith. When you have faith, you *know*. When you *know*, you annihilate fear.

New perspectives. When I feel overwhelmed, I remind myself that my distress is self-created. I take a few deep breaths and say to myself that no person or event has the power to define who I am or my level of happiness. The power comes from the way I interpret people's behaviors or events.

Choose to see your separation or divorce as a catalyst for positive change. Choose to consider this challenge in your life as the opportunity to achieve your full potential. The energy you once spent on meeting your spouse's demands or on saving your marriage is now free currency to be spent on your spiritual growth and happiness. Each day, ask yourself how you can grow into a better person because of your experience, and act upon the changes you need to make.

Choose to see your separation and divorce as a result. Not a "good" or "bad" result, just a result. Understand that your responses to events and behaviors aligned you with the breakdown of your marriage.

Finally, choose to see the innocence in your spouse, and release him or her with love so that your spouse can find his or her own path.

Quoting Lao Tzu, "One day your loss may be your fortune, one day your fortune may be your loss."[2] Choose to see the fortune in your misfortune.

CHAPTER 13

Patience
Your Thousand-Mile Journey

"The journey of a thousand miles begins with a single step."
—Lao Tzu

You probably wanted to fix your marriage. Now. Then, when you realized the marriage was not fixable, you wanted to feel better. Now.

It might not be that simple. Patience is one of your greatest allies during and after separation or divorce, and this patience must be directed toward yourself. Patience equals self-love and acceptance. Patience equals awareness of the negative emotions that might come your way. Patience equals *trusting* that you will survive. Trusting that you'll survive means surrendering your problems to the Highest Power, a concept we studied in Chapter 8.

My support group described the journey through separation and divorce as the perfect example of a so-called emotional roller coaster. One day you might feel as though you're finally stepping out of your low-energy pit, only to be hit with a new wave of grief or anger. However, you'll notice that as your spiritual growth progresses, the ups and downs will be less intense and less frequent, so that when you let yourself sink to a low-energy place, you're able to bounce back a lot faster.

Best of all, when you grow spiritually, you'll become aware of the doings of your ego. Your awareness will give you the power to dissolve your thoughts of sadness, anger, and the other negative emotions. If you had been fully engulfed by the ego, you wouldn't have been able to tame disconnection, attachment, resistance, and blaming. Your current knowledge has already brought you to a better and higher spiritual place. Your awareness is your guaranteed exit pass out of despair.

Let's examine how to apply patience in situations pertaining to separation and divorce, such as:

Adopting different routines. You'll either have more activities to manage if you have children and no help to take care of them, or have extra free time if you don't have children. Be kind to yourself as you adjust to the "new normal." You might make mistakes. You might have to make more changes until you're comfortable with your new schedule. It's okay.

Remember that palm trees are able to survive the strongest storms because they're flexible and bend in the direction of fierce winds. Be flexible as the winds of your own life slam against you. As they were for me, evenings might be the most difficult for you. Engage in evening activities that provide you with a sense of purpose, and then modify your schedule as your spiritual growth progresses.

Expanding your social connections. Friends who knew you and your spouse as a couple might stop contacting you, and married friends might keep their distance because they see you as a threat to their own marriages. Be patient as you develop friendships with a new group of people who truly value you for who you are, and allow your new relationships to grow and evolve at their own pace.

It took me over a year to start meeting people with whom I was able to establish a good connection. I knew the right people would come into my life at the right time.

Also, it's important not to force yourself to date again just so you can "move on." Moving on does not mean you switch partners; it means you emotionally detach from the need to be romantically involved with anyone to be at peace. If you haven't learned how to be happy on your own, you won't be happy with a new partner.

Avoid falling into the trap of thinking you're "getting old" and therefore must find someone new as fast as possible. Women who are nearing the end of their childbearing years tend to feel this way. Remember that when anxiety becomes part of the equation, the ego takes over and blocks your attempt to materialize your desires.

Making career changes. If you were a stay-at-home parent or worked part-time during your marriage, it's likely that you'll need to get a new job to boost your income. Keep an open mind about going back to school or joining professional groups that will lead you to the career path of your choice. If your finances are in jeopardy and you need to take the first job available, do the best you can at this new job and know that a better position will come in time because of your alignment with your Highest Self.

Moving. You might have to move to a new home, or even to a new town or state. Getting used to your new living environment and neighbors might take time. I resented putting our house up for sale and having to move. People would ask me how I liked my new place, and I would reluctantly answer that it was "okay," but that I missed my house. I actually resented being asked this question because I assumed everyone should already know how sad it had been for me to move. In my mind, my new house represented the end of my marriage.

I extracted myself from this negative energy by listing the positive aspects of the new location, and by giving thanks for having a place to live. I told myself that in time I would adjust, and six months after moving, my new place finally felt like home.

Changing the way you spend your free time. If you share custody of your children with your spouse, you'll have entire weekends/ weekdays on your own. If you don't have children, you'll have all weekends to yourself. It might take time for you to discover activities that are enjoyable and fulfilling, so be patient as you experiment with new events in your life and join new groups. What truly matters is that you use your time to do what you enjoy rather than to wallow in negative energy.

Cherish this time of exploration, and value any downtime you might have. Take your time alone to reflect on your connection with God and listen for guidance.

Regardless of the specific changes in your life, tackle them one day at a time and trust that results will arrive in divine order. As Master Saint Germain says in *The "I Am" Discourses,* "Do not become impatient because things do not work out as rapidly as you would like them to. They can only work according to the speed of your acceptance and the intensity of your feeling."[1]

Check that the actions you intend to take are aligned with your Highest Self by asking yourself if you feel good making these decisions. If your intuition says to stay away from something or from someone, do so. Make sure you differentiate between intuition and fear, however. In my experience, an intuitive thought comes as an immediate response to a situation before your conscious mind has the opportunity to react, while fear-driven thoughts tend to appear after a period of analysis.

If you're not sure whether the inner voice you hear comes from truth or fear, patiently wait until you feel at peace. The truth will eventually come to you.

CHAPTER 14

Meditation
Your Calm Revolution

"A quiet mind is all you need.
All else will happen rightly, once your mind is quiet."
—Sri Nisargadatta Maharaj

Meditation is the door to accessing the wisdom of your subconscious mind. Meditation is a form of prayer through which you can make conscious contact with God.

You might have tried meditating in the past, and judged the outcome as a failure because you couldn't get rid of all your thoughts or because you fell asleep. You might have been successful at calming your stream of thoughts for a minute, and then returned to focusing on stressful thoughts when you remembered your mile-long to-do list.

Let's clarify six myths about meditation so you can start enjoying its benefits.

Meditation doesn't require emptying your mind of all thoughts. In fact, completely freeing the mind of all thoughts is nearly impossible for most human beings. If you resist the thoughts, more thoughts will enter your mind. Thinking about not having any thoughts is a thought.

View contemplation as a type of meditation. Sometimes, by becoming a witness to your situation and weighing your options, you'll receive the guidance and peace you need.

Meditation doesn't need to last a specific amount of time. You could take two minutes to meditate while you wait in line at the grocery store, five minutes before you go to sleep, or a half-day during a meditation retreat.

Meditation doesn't need to happen in a dark room with incense and silky cushions. The place where you meditate has no impact on the quality of your meditation as long as you're inspired to make conscious contact with the Divine within you. Try meditating at a park, by the ocean, or anywhere close to nature (God's creation).

Meditation doesn't require complete silence. We explored the power of being in silence to clean your connection to the Divine, and quiet meditations tend to be some of the most powerful experiences. However, chanting a mantra or listening intently to soothing music is an effective method of meditation for millions of people, and it can be for you, too.

Meditation doesn't require physical stillness. You might prefer a walking meditation, in which your awareness is placed on the motion of your body and on your immediate environment. With this type of meditation, you find God in every noise, smell, and image around you.

Meditation doesn't have a set schedule. Depending on your mood, you might prefer to meditate in the morning when you wake up, during your lunch break, or before you go to sleep.

Now that we know what meditation is not, let's explore what meditation is.

Meditation is transcending all physical limitations. When you meditate, the physical state of your body is irrelevant. You might be physically tired or suffer from illness, but your Highest Self is always in radiant health. As you advance in your practice, you'll notice how all the aches and physical discomforts that you might have been experiencing disappear while you are in a meditative state.

Meditation is achieving a sense of inner peace. Thoughts about your separation or divorce might enter your mind during meditation, but they won't trigger negative emotions. You'll become a witness to your thoughts and detach from the effect they would otherwise have had on you.

Meditation is listening to the voice of God. When you make conscious contact with God, you'll receive the answers you seek. The answer might be a sense of joy or peace, or an idea that seems to come out of nowhere, which allows you to make an important decision. Your intuition is free to act during meditation. Listen to it. And if the answer to your question doesn't come during a specific session, then trust that it will come to you in time.

Meditation is being in the now. Though meditation can happen even when there are thoughts in your head, it's important that you bring your awareness to the present moment. Placing your attention on past hurts or the uncertainty of your future will prevent you from making conscious contact with the Divine.

Meditation is an act of self-love. By taking the time to meditate, you're saying to yourself and to the universe that you matter. By meditating, you're sending out this silent affirmation: *I am magnificent.*

The way to meditate is a personal choice. What really matters is that you set aside time every day to make conscious contact with God. I practice several forms of meditation depending on how I feel on a specific day, but I find that it's easier for me to meditate upon awakening, when there are no distractions.

When you begin to meditate on a regular basis, you'll receive answers to those questions that once kept you up at night. You'll let go of the low-energy feelings that paralyzed you because you'll feel the presence of God inside you. Like any practice, meditation requires dedication and commitment. In time, meditating will become second nature to you, and you'll undergo a calm, but extremely powerful, revolution in your life.

PART FOUR

The Power of Your Highest Self

CHAPTER 15

Synchronicity
Tapping into the Power of
Your Highest Self

"Meaningful coincidences are thinkable as pure chance.
But the more they multiply and the greater and more exact
the correspondence is, the more their probability sinks and
their unthinkability increases, until they can no longer be
regarded as pure chance but, for lack of a causal explanation,
have to be thought of as meaningful arrangements."
—Carl Jung

You've learned how to raise your level of awareness. You've learned how to tame your ego. You've explored the tools to help you heal and manifest happiness. It's been quite a journey, but you're here. You're ready to tap into the power of your Highest Self through synchronicity.

What exactly is synchronicity? First, let's examine the concept of coincidence. You probably experience coincidences all the time. You're thinking about someone and he calls you, or you see someone you hadn't seen in ten years, and the next day you see him again. You might have dismissed these related events that seem to have no cause or effect over the other as appearing "by chance," and called them *coincidences.* However, in a universe where everything is divinely orchestrated, what seem to be unrelated events are occurring as a reflection of the subconscious mind at work.

All coincidences have meaning, but this meaning might not be evident in many cases. There are no accidents, only unawareness of the forces driving everything that takes form.

How are coincidences and synchronicity related? I would define *synchronicity* as a coincidence with a clear meaning, and the meaning is only clear to you when your connection with your Highest Self is pure and clean. Occurrence A does not cause occurrence B. A and B happen as the result of your alignment with the Divine. Synchronicity is a magnificent power, and the ultimate step in your healing and self-realization process.

When you experience synchronicity, healing from your separation or divorce will be only an added benefit. Synchronicity will open the door to a path of enlightenment. Miraculous things will start happening in your life. You'll be guided to the places you needed to go, and will meet the people you needed to meet. You'll come across a book or a website that holds the answers to your questions. Goodness will effortlessly flow into your life, but you won't be surprised, because you'll have an inner knowing that this is the Divine within you in action.

Regardless of your current life circumstances, you'll be aligned with high-energy thoughts and emotions and will reject negative emotions for what they are: unreal. The universal mind will respond to your alignment with high-energy fields by providing you with additional positive experiences.

You'll be able to see your spouse for who he or she truly is, and to move toward authentic, divine love for the first time. You'll feel connected to God, to other people, and to your spouse. You'll be able to let go of your attachments and become free to experience happiness. You'll surrender to the power of God when you're not sure what to do or wonder what the future might bring. You'll assume responsibility for everything that has happened or is happening in your life, including your separation or divorce.

The power of your imagination will be brought into form. There will be a clear picture in your head of the life you want to live, and you'll have already experienced this life in your body, because you will have assumed the feeling of your wishes fulfilled. Instead of just knowing about healing and happiness, you'll *know* healing and happiness.

You'll be able to deflect negative outcomes using the power of your intuition, because you'll learn to step ahead of those outcomes.

Your mind will be open to the abundance that life has to offer. Rigidity will not be a factor in your life, and you'll experience exciting and enriching activities and relationships.

You'll behave in ways that match the fulfilling life you have imagined, but if the results you expect don't materialize within your expected timeframe, you'll have no problem waiting. You'll trust that everything happens in divine order.

God will speak to you through meditation and even during your daily activities. You won't need a special time and place to realize your connection to the Divine.

Being connected to your Highest Self at all times is something that only an avatar of God, such as Jesus, has accomplished. Your ego will still surface, but you'll catch yourself before sinking into low-energy fields. The self-imposed barriers of your past will gradually break down as your connection with your Highest Self strengthens.

The new programs in your subconscious mind will manifest themselves in subtle, yet powerful ways. You might find yourself feeling happy for no reason. You might notice that you didn't think about your situation or your spouse for hours or even days. You might feel light inside, as though someone filled your lungs with a special, blessed form of oxygen. The internal transformation that you'll experience can't be stopped, but will grow in an avalanche of increased joy and sense of purpose. You'll start experiencing and effecting miracles, which are nothing more than expressions of synchronicity.

I have experienced synchronicity throughout the writing of this book. Every time I experience it, I elevate myself to a higher level of awareness.

Now, when I look back at my three-year journey, I realize that every time my low-energy feelings took over, I found myself void of synchronicity. I felt lost. It was only when I regained my connection to God and raised my energy levels that the so-called coincidental occurrences resumed. That's when I understood that being attached to my husband and to our marriage was preventing me from tapping into the divine power I already possessed. That's when I made the conscious decision to let go. By doing so, I experienced a complete shift in my perception and a dramatic increase in my conscious awareness.

It was only when I decided to surrender to the power of God that I was inspired to write this book so I could touch your life and help you as you travel your own path of self-discovery. I send you all my love and blessings during this time in your life. My heart is with you.

APPENDIX A

Tricky Situations

The following pages offer guidance on topics that require special attention because of their potential to trigger a cascade of negative thoughts and emotions in your conscious self. I'd like to remind you that in reality, none of these situations has power to affect you negatively, but your current subconscious programming might make them seem to be the most challenging in the continuum of the separation and divorce process.

Dealing with Attorneys

If you're separated and considering divorce, you and your spouse have consulted, or will consult, attorneys. If you're in the process of divorce, each of you is most likely represented by an attorney. If you have already divorced, attorney intervention might still be needed for post-judgment alimony adjustments and distribution of assets that weren't readily available at the time of divorce (sale of your home, stock options, and so on).

Bottom line, attorneys will enter your life during this time of transition, and you need to make sure that these attorneys do not threaten your sense of connection and peace.

Attorney Selection

Even if you've already selected your attorney, I urge you to realize that you're entitled to change your selection if the attorney's methods don't match your values. You can switch attorneys even if you are already in the midst of the divorce process. If your choice of attorney is not the best for you, but you tell yourself that you "have invested too much in the attorney" or that "it's too much work," or wonder "what the attorney might think," you're subconsciously responding to your attachment to the way things are and to what people think of you. The sooner you switch attorneys, the more cost effective and smoother the transition to working with your new attorney will be.

The following suggestions apply if you're in the process of selecting an attorney or if you already have an attorney, but feel unsure whether that attorney is the best fit for you.

List your values on paper. If reaching your Highest Self is your ultimate destination, one of your top values will be peace.

Interview at least three attorneys. During these interviews, pay attention to the attorneys' choice of words and body language. Your intuition will tell you if they have your best interests in mind rather than the desire to "win" in an adversarial divorce. Be aware of how you feel during your conversations. If you feel good (God), the attorney is a good choice. If you feel nervous sweat trickling down your arms or an urge to run out of the lawyer's office, it's best to move on.

Consider changing attorneys if:

- The lawyer mostly handles criminal cases or other cases in which trials are involved. This shows this person's preference for adversarial cases.
- The lawyer makes statements that damage your self-esteem. You feel incompetent or ignorant when you talk to this lawyer.
- The lawyer makes comments that deny expectations for a peaceful resolution.

- The lawyer jokes about divorcing couples wanting to "kill each other" (this actually happened to me) or says that "peaceful agreement is rare." You know how the universe works: If the lawyer cannot visualize the achievement of a peaceful resolution, the peaceful resolution has no chance of happening.

Conducting Peaceful Negotiations

Negotiation involves everything from retirement account distribution, to child custody and who takes what piece of furniture. When negotiating, you need to be prepared to be like water: adaptable, but strong—especially in determining your financial rights.

Paradoxically, effective negotiators are not attached to the material possessions for which they negotiate. They know that only by letting go of these attachments can they clear their minds to decide what concessions they're willing to make.

Internal clues to determine if you're attached to the material goods you must negotiate for are that:

- You sink to lower levels of energy when presented with the possibility of material belongings being taken away from you.
- You believe you *need* those material things to be at peace.

The first step to nullify your material attachments is to be aware of ego-created thoughts during the negotiation process.

Let's say there's a recliner in your living room that your spouse wants to take, but you refuse to allow him or her to take it because it's *your* recliner and you *need* it, even if you don't remember the last time you sat on it. You might also think your spouse shouldn't be allowed to take anything that is even slightly appealing to you because it's your spouse's fault that the marriage is ending. That's your ego blaming external circumstances and seeking revenge. When you catch yourself having these thoughts, you can quickly replace them with thoughts aligned with Spirit.

You also need to learn to differentiate between attachment to the material and satisfaction of your financial needs. Proposing a financial agreement that allows you to cover the entirety of your expenses and to achieve an equitable division of assets is not an ego-driven behavior. However, if you start feeling anxious about achieving this fair agreement, or are afraid of the uncertainty of your financial future, you'll be letting in the ego. Catch yourself before the negative emotions take over, and you'll have a much more peaceful negotiation process.

Negotiation Stages

Let's talk about how to respect and preserve your connection with your spouse at the beginning, during, and after the negotiation process.

Beginning the Negotiation Process

Start by researching every item on the divorce agreement. You might be tempted to put the research off, figuring that your situation might turn around and you won't have to get divorced. Put this excuse aside and realize that the agreement represents your future, and your children's financial future, so being well informed is essential.

Next, tally all your household expenses. Include the major categories first: mortgage, utilities, food, health, clothing, insurance. Add the smaller expenses by reviewing your checking account or credit card statements. Think of this exercise as beneficial to you because it'll allow you to have a good handle on how much money you spend so you can better manage your finances.

Organize your financial documents: tax forms, bank account statements, mortgage statements, and the like. This task might be tedious, but you can choose to see it as an empowering way to gain control of your finances.

Research divorce laws in your state so you know what to expect in asset division and custody.

Complete all research and organization tasks when you feel emotionally strong. Visualize yourself easily finding the information you need and you'll be guided to the right sources of that information. Once you've found it, set it aside until you need it. Avoid rehashing worries about your finances or playing dreadful scenarios of the future in your head.

During the Negotiation Process

The midst of the negotiation is when you and your spouse might be most vulnerable to negative energies. Remember that regardless of your spouse's behavior you can control your own thoughts and behaviors. You can choose to steer the process away from negativity. To remain connected to your spouse during negotiation means to bring your light to all the dark places that might surface during the discussions. If you do so, your influence will be so strong, yet so subtle, that any darkness brought up by greed, anger, and fear will disappear.

When my attorney released the first draft of the divorce agreement, my husband was livid. He even threatened to quit his job so he wouldn't have to be responsible for alimony. Instead of returning anger in response to his anger, I waited for him to finish expressing his feelings and then told him my only goal was peace. I told him I cared about him so deeply that I would never do anything that would be unfair to him. I meant what I said. His anger was diffused. I followed with an email restating my intention, which positively influenced his perception of the fairness of the process. I delivered on my promise by discussing and redefining the terms of the agreement with my attorney.

I was presented with many more opportunities to diffuse fear and anger. I continued firmly aligning myself with peace, and even though I experienced symptoms of stress, I was successful in settling the terms of the agreement with my husband outside the court and without additional attorney intervention.

Suggestions for a Peaceful Negotiation Process

Wait before replying to email or text messages. Many times, the tone of your spouse's emails will seem offensive. Ask yourself whether you are interpreting the tone of the messages based on the negative emotions you are carrying. If you let your emotions rule and immediately send an angry reply, you'll add more fuel to the tension between you and your spouse. I suggest you draft a reply and review it when you feel calm. Most of the time, you'll want to edit the message. This small step can make a huge difference in the quality of the connection you establish with your spouse.

Favor face-to-face meetings. Face-to-face meetings allow you to use and read body language, which is the most significant element in communication. Negotiating on the phone is likely to result in miscommunication and increased frustration because reaching an agreement will probably take longer. Also, by being in the physical presence of your spouse, you'll be able to "see" in him or her the person you shared an important part of your life with, which will make it easier to approach your interactions with compassion and understanding.

Listen. Good listening skills involve receiving the messages from your spouse with an open mind, and sending thoughts of judgment away. Listening also involves empathy. Spouses who have walked away from their marriages usually carry a heavy load of guilt, shame, fear, anger, and distress. Communicate with your spouse in a way that will allow him or her to step out of those low energy levels.

Also, take the time you need to digest your spouse's requests before giving an answer, whether the answer is to agree or disagree with his or her proposal. Knee-jerk negative reactions might come across as a lack of caring and an unwillingness to understand and compromise. If you quickly agree without weighing the consequences, you might want to change your mind later, which will erode any goodwill you might have earned, and will extend the negotiation process.

Nullify revenge. Revenge might pop into your head more than once. Your conscious mind might come up with creative ways to make your spouse and anyone else who hurt you "pay." The truth is that you'll also pay when you choose revenge. On David Hawkins' scale of human consciousness, the emotions stirred by revenge had some of the lowest calibrations on the spectrum, and whoever sought revenge experienced extreme physical weakness and energy depletion.

Being connected to your Highest Self doesn't allow room for revenge. When you are in touch with the Divine inside you, you'll have no judgment or need to make things "right." You'll flow along the path that lies ahead of you without a glance back.

Here are suggestions to nullify three expressions of revenge that might have popped into your head, even if your ego masquerades the desire for revenge as "being fair."

- *Monetary revenge.* Your cultural programming, which emphasizes lawsuits and monetary compensation for "pain and suffering," might make you feel entitled to excess material goods during the unwanted divorce as a way to "get even." Identify this attitude as a driver of negative energy, and instead focus on keeping only the assets you need to be financially secure. Use your research to back up your financial requests.

  If you demand more to "get even," you will waste money and time in court, and even if you "win" and are awarded extra money, you'll feel like a loser. You'll realize that your happiness wasn't housed in the amount of money you received. You might become a bitter person who happens to have more money.

- *Revenge through the children.* Many people seek revenge by preventing their spouses from seeing the children, or by demanding sole custody of the children. The negative energy behind these actions will spread to your children and will impact their emotional development. As long as there's no history of abuse, your children will most likely benefit from time spent with both parents. If you wish to limit the time that your children are with your spouse, make sure you're basing your request on the best interest of the children, and not on the best interest of your ego.

- *Revenge through badmouthing.* It might be tempting to tell anyone you meet what a terrible person your spouse turned out to be. You might itch to talk about how your spouse became a stranger, betrayed you, abused you, and so forth. But the more you badmouth your spouse, the more you'll sink into low energy levels, which will bring about more of the same low energy, and will block the realization of your true, Highest Self.

Badmouthing is the harshest form of judgment, and judgment results in more judgment. Instead of badmouthing your spouse, I suggest verbalizing your feelings about him or her when you are alone. Imagine your spouse is sitting in front of you, and express to him or her how you feel. This strategy proved cathartic and healing for me. I also suggest bringing light to the darkness of judgment by writing down all the positive aspects of your marriage, what you learned from your spouse, and all the attributes that you admire in your spouse. You might decide to share this information with your spouse if the nature of your relationship after divorce allows for it.

Sometimes, the strength of your connection to Spirit will be tested. Forgive yourself if you fail, and return to the path to reaching your Highest Self as soon as you can. Although being connected to Spirit is paramount when life is going your way and when people are being good to you, it's even more important when circumstances don't turn out the way you want and when people hurt you.

Here is a final checklist to determine if your role in the negotiation process is aligned with high-level energy.

- You are fully disclosing all financial information.
- You have a clear understanding of your financial needs.
- Your monetary demands are solely based on your children's and your financial security.
- Your child custody demands are based on the well-being of your children.
- You focus on the present moment during the negotiation process, and not on past hurts or fear about the future.
- You feel good about the process. Remember, when you feel good, you feel God.

After the Negotiation Process

Once you and your spouse have come to an agreement, you need to continue being like water; flowing softly but powerfully down the path to a life on your own. This means:

- *Committing to what you have agreed.* Your negative emotions might return and prompt you to think you gave in too easily. If your decision was backed with diligent research and done with objectivity, you can rest assured the agreement in your hands is the best for you.
- *Keeping the details of your agreement private, especially when in the company of close relatives and friends.* These people care about you, but their definition of caring might

include viewing your spouse as the enemy, so they might encourage you to be "tougher" because you "deserve" more financial assets after what you've gone through. They might also tell you the story of someone who received a much better financial settlement than you, awakening your ego's need to be better than everyone else. Be aware of ego-driven thoughts as they appear, and allow time to pass before reacting to after-settlement comments or unsolicited advice.

- *Staying organized.* You are now responsible for your own finances, so you'll need to keep close track of the execution of the agreement. Commit to sticking to your financial budget.
- *Checking how you feel.* When the final agreement is in your hands and after you've put aside any negative thoughts driven by fear, you'll feel good. Then you'll know you're connected to God.

Remarrying Your Ex-Spouse

You've probably considered this possibility at least once during the process of divorce. Depending on your emotional state, you might have said to yourself:

- "Never!"
- "Maybe."
- "Only if my spouse makes the changes he or she needs to make."
- "Of course!"

Your opinion might have changed more than once; even daily. Your ex-spouse, even though he or she was the one to leave, might have also toyed with the possibility of future reconciliation.

It's healthy to have an open mind and consider the possibility of getting back together with your ex-spouse in the future, but it isn't healthy to make your happiness dependent on the realization of this possibility.

Also, spend some time in quiet contemplation to determine if you're seeing what you want to see instead of what it's true. A future with your ex-spouse might not be in your best interest. Maybe you were emotionally abused or were prevented from living a meaningful life, but you don't see it because your only goal is to get back together with your spouse. Maybe you're attached to the idea that you married your soul mate and you're destined to be together, but the truth is that you were in a toxic relationship that ended for valid reasons.

Before considering the idea of remarriage, it's essential that you place yourself on the path to a clean connection to your Highest Self, so you can access divine guidance before making such a decision. If you remain aligned with your Highest Self, you'll be aligned with future reconciliation only if it's in your best interest. If the answer you receive during meditation is to say no to reconciliation, honor it. Follow divine guidance even if your ex-spouse expresses interest in reconciling.

Here are some examples of how a strong and clean connection with your Highest Self before and during divorce would allow for the possibility of future reconciliation.

- *You handle the divorce process in an amicable manner.* You listen to your spouse's requests without judgment, and you have enough confidence to stand up for what you believe is fair financially. Once the divorce is finalized, both you and your ex-partner feel respected and acknowledged.
- *You consider the needs of your children when arranging child custody, and disregard any impulse to "get back" at your spouse in this process.* There's no custody battle, and you're able to co-parent effectively without bringing in additional negative emotions.
- *You don't badmouth your ex-spouse to your children, relatives, and friends.* The relationships between your spouse and your family and the people in your social circles remain as positive as possible.

- *You decide to forgive your ex-spouse for leaving the marriage, and send him or her out of your life with love.* In the future, if your ex-spouse has a change of heart, he or she is the one to reach out to you because he or she feels that you don't harbor hate and don't see him or her in a negative light.
- *Your alignment with high-energy fields raises the energy of everyone around you, including your ex-spouse.* He or she feels relaxed around you and is encouraged to be friendly and open.
- *You become a much better person than you used to be.* This is attractive not only to your ex-spouse, but to other future romantic partners.

Keep in mind that in cases in which physical or emotional abuse and/or addiction issues were present, reconciling might not be in your best interest. As I mentioned before, this is why it's so important that you establish a clean connection with your Highest Self before even considering reconciliation. Let your divine power guide you as you make your decision.

Handling Separation and Divorce "Milestones"

Some days on the continuum of your separation or divorce will seem to be a lot harder to get through than others, and might trigger a long chain of negative emotions.

Examples of these situations are:

- Your spouse's move.
- The first meeting with a family attorney.
- Your spouse's announcement that he or she wants a divorce.
- Your spouse filing for divorce.
- Being served divorce papers.
- Communicating with friends and family that you and your spouse are ending your marriage.

- Putting your house on the market.
- Selling your home.
- Moving out of your home.
- The day prior to your divorce date.
- The final court hearing date.
- The first day your children spend with your spouse and away from you.
- The first day your children visit your spouse's new place.
- The first time someone asks if you're married and your answer is no.
- The day you hear your spouse or ex-spouse is romantically involved with someone else.
- Your wedding anniversary.
- Your birthday.
- Your spouse's birthday.
- The children's birthdays.
- Special holidays.

The list goes on and on.

If you experience debilitating feelings when faced with the milestones listed, I urge you to realize that the root cause is your thoughts about these singular situations in the context of separation or divorce. Your spouse moving out or filing for divorce, or any other situation, has no power over you except what you allow. The proof is that if you came home from work and didn't know your spouse had moved out, you would be fine.

If your spouse filed for divorce and you didn't know about it for two weeks, you would continue living your life during those two weeks as though nothing had happened. If your spouse was romantically involved with someone for months and you didn't know it, you would be okay. When your mind registers the information and compares it to the programming in your subconscious mind, you think you *need* to feel negative emotions, so you do. Even though it might seem impossible, you have the power to choose thoughts that will strengthen you instead of weaken you, and the choice is available to you now.

Here are strategies to cope with these milestones.

- *When a thought that unchains negative reactions hits you, replace it with an empowering counterpart.* For example, if you think you'll never be able to overcome the situation, tell yourself that you'll get through the next hour or through the day, and once the hour or the day has passed, you will reevaluate. Breaking huge undertakings into smaller pieces will allow you to alter your perspective. It all comes down to changing the way you look at your situation.

- *Avoid bottling up the negative feelings or fighting them if they have already appeared.* Allow the feelings to flow. Remember that resisting them will intensify them. Allow the tears to come. Find comfort in the words of a friend. Then, during meditation, surrender the negative feelings to the Highest Power.

- *Become even more diligent about your meditation practice to achieve a daily conscious connection with your Highest Self.*

- *Start new traditions. If* you used to have a home-cooked meal on your child's birthday, go out to a restaurant. If you always went away for Thanksgiving, stay home. Treasure these new traditions and focus on the blessings you're given on each occasion.

- *If you wake up in the middle of the night with thoughts of anxiety or fear, turn on a soft light.* Bring physical light into the darkness and recognize that there's nothing out there that can hurt you except your own thoughts about the situation. Take deep breaths and ask God for guidance.

- *Take time off from work if your job is very demanding.* Even leaving a couple of hours early to take care of yourself will have a profound beneficial effect.

- *Carve out time for walks in nature and time with close friends and family.* If you feel like you need a hug, ask for it.

- *If you find yourself unable to snap out of your grief, reach out to help others.* Giving will immediately place you in conscious contact with God, who always gives. Your ego will be tamed by the presence of high-level energy.
- *Reread the sections of this book that most resonated with you.*

How long will the despair last? I don't have the answer. Only you do.

Dealing with "Someone Waiting in the Wings"

Dealing with your spouse's romantic relationship with another person can intensify the range and duration of your low-energy emotions. The reason is that your ego is doubly wounded. First, your marriage is ending. Second, you're being "replaced" with another person. The ego sees the other person as a clear violation of your territory (your spouse) and as proof that there's something wrong with you. The ego then shifts the blame onto the other person, sometimes releasing the spouse who has left from all blame.

There are four basic situations that you might face.

Scenario 1. The relationship started before your spouse left, and you blame the other person for breaking up your marriage. Your spouse might have moved out after the affair came to light, whether it was his or her own initiative to move or you requested it. If you were the one to ask your spouse to move out, you might feel extreme anger for the betrayal, and guilt for having asked your spouse to leave. If your spouse moved out to be with the other person, you might still experience intense anger, but also a strong sense of being unworthy (not good enough). Regardless of who took the initiative, I invite you to consider the following:

- *Assume responsibility for the affair, even if your spouse was the one to stray.* Somehow, even if subconsciously, you aligned yourself with the betrayal, and by owning what

173

happened, you'll have the power to stop it from hurting you further. This step was the most challenging for me, but once I was able to own the situation, I felt more in control of my emotions.

- *Your divine nature is not dependent on your spouse's behavior.* The fact that you were left for someone else doesn't mean that you are less of a person or that the other person has greater value.

- *If you asked your spouse to move out, remember that your decision was what you thought you had to do given the circumstances in your life and your emotional state.* The decision is in the past, and you need to focus on eliminating the self-imposed guilt that's preventing you from living a realized life. If there's an opportunity to reconsider your decision, then give it some thought, but make sure you are patient with yourself and give yourself the time necessary to keep or to change the decision. Wait until guilt is not part of the equation to reevaluate, and remember that changing your decision isn't a sign of weakness, but proof that you're in touch with your Highest Self.

- *Forgiveness might take a moment or take years, but in the end, the act of forgiveness will release you from the grasp of negative emotions, and will free you to make conscious contact with the Divine.* As you have already learned, forgiveness is not the same as forgetting what happened or "being a doormat." Forgiveness doesn't mean letting your spouse and the other person disrespect you or mistreat you. Forgiveness means that your thoughts about your spouse's and his or her lover's actions no longer immobilize you. Be patient with yourself as you move toward that forgiveness.

Scenario 2. The relationship started after your spouse moved out, but before divorce papers were filed. This situation might also bring a deep sense of anger, of being out of control, and of worthlessness. You might blame your spouse for reckless behavior and for not respecting that you're still married. You might find yourself wondering where your spouse met the other person, and create stories in your head about your spouse taking the other person to the places you used to frequent as a couple. You'll probably picture your spouse being physically intimate with the other person and as a result, experience physical symptoms of malaise. I know first-hand how sickening these thoughts can be.

To weaken the effect these thoughts have on you, I invite you to reflect on the following ideas.

- *Your spouse is doing what he or she thinks is right given his or her cultural programming and emotional circumstances.* A spouse who has left often feels that the marriage is over, and feels entitled to "date" other people. Your spouse might believe that once he or she is not living under the same roof as you, there are no marital obligations to keep.
- *You cannot expect your spouse to act in the same way that you would act, and you cannot control his or her actions.* Practice surrendering this situation over which you have no control, and focus on controlling your own thoughts and actions so you're aligned with faster and higher energies. My judgments toward my husband would always start with the thought that "I would have never done" such and such. Whatever I would have done didn't really matter, because I wasn't the one who had taken action.
- *When feelings of being worthless appear, remind yourself of your divine nature.*
- *Realize that there's a possibility that your marriage will end and also a possibility that it will be saved.* Place your attention on the outcome that is aligned with your Highest Self, but don't become attached to this outcome, because your motives will be then driven by your ego.

Scenario 3. The relationship started after divorce papers were filed, but before the divorce was final. My previous statement about your spouse's programming still applies to this situation. For many people, filing for divorce is equal to being divorced. Your spouse might feel free to explore relationships with other people openly and publicly. Some of the people in my support group found themselves dealing with Facebook pictures of their spouses and their new romantic partners posted by their spouses themselves, and with their spouses changing their relationship status as "single" or "in a relationship." Some of my friends saw their spouses' active online dating profiles. Others had to deal with their spouses wanting the children to meet their new "boyfriend" or "girlfriend."

My suggestion is that you remain keenly aware of the root cause of your emotions. All feelings of anger and worthlessness stem from your ego. Surrendering the situation to God is paramount. If you decide to focus on the possibility that your marriage might still be saved, don't allow your ego's attachment to the outcome paralyze you or steer you away from the path to reaching your Highest Self.

Scenario 4. The relationship starts shortly after the divorce is final. The fact that you've signed a paper saying that you are divorced might not make a difference in your feelings and level of attachment to the relationship with your spouse. If you're still strongly attached to the desire to reconcile with your ex-spouse and find out that he or she is in a new romantic relationship, the low-energy thoughts and feelings you experienced before and during the divorce might resurface. My suggestion is to reflect on the following ideas.

- *If you still wish for reconciliation after divorce, make sure you keep your ego at bay by not becoming emotionally attached to the outcome.* As long as you are not immobilized and wasting the present moment because of your aspiration to reconcile, you'll still be able to live a self-actualized life.
- *You can continue loving your ex-spouse after divorce, but your love doesn't mean that you're entitled to control his or her life or to exert control over his or her actions.* Love means seeing people as they are and allowing them to choose

the path that they desire, regardless of your opinion about this path or your presence in it.

- *If your ex-spouse and you are great co-parents, this doesn't mean your ex-spouse will be open to reconciliation.* Continue collaborating to raise your children in a loving environment, but separate this role from your role as a husband or wife. Be aware that your children will probably meet and spend time with your ex-spouse's new romantic partner.
- *Surrender your low-energy thoughts and feelings to God.* If you keep the connection with your Highest Self strong and pure, you'll be guided to where you need to go.

APPENDIX B

Ten Topics for Reflection

Below is a series of lists and questions for reflection that will help you put into practice the principles you've learned in this book. I suggest you keep all the lists together and review them when you need a reminder of your mission: to heal and to establish conscious contact with your Highest Self.

1. Name all the positive traits in your spouse and the positive acts he or she did for you during the time you were together. See your time together as a gift rather than a waste.
2. Jot down the names of all the people who have been there for you as you go through this transition. What did you learn about your relationship with each one of these people? Which relationships would you like to deepen and how can you strengthen these connections?
3. Enumerate all the ways in which you give love to others. How do you feel when you give of yourself to others? What activities offer a sense of connection to others?
4. Contemplate all the new experiences that you have had since you have been living on your own.
5. List all the experiences you want to have in the future.
6. Determine your current values. After you complete the list, assign priorities to each value, and then circle your top

five. Reevaluate this information as your spiritual growth continues, and take note of the changes.

7. Create a list of *I ams*. Include all the qualities that describe you. For example: "I am strong. I am independent. I am healthy." Add the qualities that you would like to describe you, realizing that you are already connected to those qualities and only need to allow them to manifest in your life. Use your *I am* list during your meditation practice.

8. Think of all that you did to become a better person and to save your relationship. Be at peace knowing you did everything that was in your hands at the time.

9. Keep track of all the synchronistic events in your life, even if they would seem to be mere coincidences to other people. Jot down how your connection to God manifested itself in these events.

10. Write down any messages you might receive during or after meditation, or as you awaken. These intuitive messages are from God.

Acknowledgments

My deepest gratitude to my editor, Stephanie Gunning. Your topnotch edits allowed me to offer the highest-quality product that my readers deserve.

In alphabetical order, a million thanks to Helen Bailey, Millie Grenough, Pam Grout, Elizabeth Hamilton-Guarino, Prudence Holling, Allen Klein, Hilary Topper, and Alicia Young. You encouraged me with words and actions, and showed your belief in my abilities by endorsing my book.

To my incredible radio guests and faithful readers. You inspired me to continue pursuing my true calling no matter the circumstances in my life.

To editor Jill Kramer, the first person to read my work and affirm that I'd be able to positively change the lives of many people with this book.

To my friend and copy editor, Kat Maruzak. I treasure your encouragement and enthusiasm as much as your detailed and prompt work.

To Lori Deschene, founder of TinyBuddha.com, who gave me the opportunity to share my message with millions of readers. Your feedback made my writing more engaging and compelling.

To the fabulous team at Balboa Press, whose promptness and commitment to excellence made the publishing of this book a true pleasure.

A huge thank you to all the friends and family who offered their love and support during my journey, and to my fabulous online support group. They held my hand, cried with me during the tough times, and cheered me on when I emerged from the pit of despair and started putting my ideas on paper.

To Dr. Wayne W. Dyer, my spiritual teacher. Your books, lectures, and encouragement allowed me to turn the biggest challenge in my life into a growing, life-changing experience. I will be forever grateful.

To my dear mom. I treasure the unconditional love you've given me.

To my loving dad, who might have left the earthly realm, but has never left my side.

Most of all, I thank God for allowing me to channel divine wisdom to write this book, and for the awareness that I'm never alone.

You're all magnificent, and I send you love.

Notes

Introduction

Epigraph. Viktor Frankl, *Man's Search for Meaning* (Boston, MA.: Beacon Press, 2006): p. 112.
1. Wayne Dyer, *Wishes Fulfilled* (Carlsbad, CA.: Hay House, 2012): p. 49.
2. Nikos Kazantzakis, *Saint Francis,* P.A. Bien, translator (Chicago, IL.: Loyola Press, 2005): p. 18.

Chapter 1   Your Place in the Energy Spectrum

Epigraph. Nikola Tesla. See the Goodreads website: http://www. goodreads.com/quotes/361785-if-you-want-to-find-the-secrets-of-the-universe (accessed December 11, 2013).
1. Wayne Dyer, *There's a Spiritual Solution to Every Problem* (New York: HarperCollins, 2003): p. 44.
2. David R. Hawkins, *Power vs. Force* (Carlsbad, CA.: Hay House, 2012): p. 55.

Chapter 2   Sinking into Low-Energy Fields

Epigraph. Ascended Master Saint Germain, *The "I Am" Discourses*, Volume 3, Discourse 3 (Schaumburg, IL.: Saint Germain Press, 2011).

Chapter 3   Rising to High-Energy Fields

Epigraph. Uell S. Andersen, *Three Magic Words* (New York: Snowball Publishing, 2012): p. 187.

1. James Thurber. See Brainy Quote website: http://www.brainyquote. com/quotes/quotes/j/jamesthurb106488.html (accessed December 12, 2013).

2. Henry David Thoreau. See @ThoreauPage on Twitter: https:// twitter.com/ThoreauPage/status/394579151992016896 (accessed December 12, 2013).

3. Coleman Barks, *A Year with Rumi* (New York: HarperCollins, 2006): p. 127.

4. Anthony de Mello, *The Way to Love* (New York: Doubleday, 1995): p. 106.

5. Wayne Dyer, "Success Secrets," Dr. Wayne W. Dyer blog (posted October 15, 2009): http://www.drwaynedyer.com/blog/ success-secrets.

6. Søren Kierkegaard. See Goodreads website: https://www. goodreads.com/quotes/24012-once-you-label-me-you-negate-me (accessed December 12, 2013).

7. Ancient Chinese proverb. See Searchquotes website: http:// www.searchquotes.com/quotation/He_who_seeks_vengeance_ must_dig_two_graves%3A_one_for_his_enemy_and_one_for_ himself/25287 (accessed December 12, 2013).

8. *A Course in Miracles* (Mill Valley, CA.: Foundation for Inner Peace, 2007): p. 378. The Course was originally channeled and transcribed by Helen Schucman.

9. Francois de La Rochefoucauld. See Goodreads website: https:// www.goodreads.com/quotes/213766-the-only-thing-constant-in- life-is-change (accessed December 12, 2013).

10. Uell S. Andersen, *Three Magic Words* (New York: Snowball Publishing, 2012): p. 30.

Chapter 4   Using Your Life's Currency:
The Law of Attraction

Epigraph. Neville Goddard, *The Power of Awareness* (1952) (Huey Global, 2012): p. 31.

1. Uell S. Andersen, *Three Magic Words* (New York: Snowball Publishing, 2012): p. 191.
2. James Allen, *Book of Meditations for Every Day in the Year* (1913), in *Mind Is the Master* (New York: J.P. Tarcher/Penguin, 2010): p. 762.

Chapter 5   Your Highest Self vs. Your Ego:
Always a Winning Battle

Epigraph. *A Course in Miracles* (Mill Valley, CA: Foundation for Inner Peace, 2007): p. 22.

Chapter 6   Disconnection to Connection:
Going Where You Belong

Epigraph. Herman Melville. See Goodreads website: https://www.goodreads.com/quotes/156835-we-cannot-live-only-for-ourselves-a-thousand-fibers-connect (accessed December 12, 2013).

1. *A Course in Miracles* (Mill Valley, CA.: Foundation for Inner Peace, 2007): p. 12.
2. Herman Melville, *Pierre, or The Ambiguities* (1852) (Charleston, S.C.: BiblioLife, 2011): p. 284.
3. Wayne Dyer, *Change Your Thoughts, Change Your Life* (Carlsbad, CA.: Hay House, 2007): p. 208.
4. Uell S. Andersen, *Three Magic Words* (New York: Snowball Publishing, 2012): p. 51.
5. Anthony de Mello, *The Way to Love* (New York: Doubleday, 1995): p. 34.

6. Peter Deunov, *Love Is All Forgiving* (Deerfield Beach, FL.: Health Communications, 2004).

Chapter 7   Attachment to Detachment: Breaking the Chains

Epigraph. Meister Eckhart. See Brainy Quote website: http://www. brainyquote.com/quotes/quotes/m/meistereck149148.html (accessed December 13, 2013).
1. Anthony de Mello, *Rediscovering Life* (New York: Image Books, 2012): p. 37.
2. Anthony de Mello, *The Way to Love* (New York: Doubleday, 1995): p. 43.
3. Uell S. Andersen, *Three Magic Words* (New York: Snowball Publishing, 2012): p. 29.
4. Anthony de Mello, *Rediscovering Life* (New York: Image Books, 2012): p. 42
5. Kahlil Gibran. See Brainy Quote website: http://www.brainyquote. com/quotes/quotes/k/khalilgibr166623.html (accessed December 12, 2013).
6. David Hawkins, *The Eye of the I* (kindle edition) (West Sedona, AZ.: Veritas Publishing, 2010).
7. *A Course in Miracles* (Mill Valley, CA: Foundation for Inner Peace, 2007): p. 85.
8. Ralph Waldo Emerson. See Brainy Quote website: http:// www.brainyquote.com/quotes/quotes/r/ralphwaldo136909.html (accessed December 12, 2013).

Chapter 8   Resistance vs. Allowing: Letting Go

Epigraph. Lao Tzu, as quoted by Wayne Dyer, *Change Your Thoughts, Change Your Life* (Carlsbad, CA.: Hay House, 2007): p. 104.
1. See Wikipedia website: http://en.wikipedia.org/wiki/K%C3% BCbler-Ross_model (accessed December 12, 2013).

Chapter 9   Blaming vs. Taking Ownership:
Reclaiming Your Power

Epigraph. Dwight D. Eisenhower. See Goodreads website: http://www.goodreads.com/quotes/43785-the-search-for-a-scapegoat-is-the-easiest-of-all (accessed December 13, 2013).

Chapter 10   Your Imagination: The Power of Your
Subconscious Mind

Epigraph. Pablo Picasso. See Goodreads website: http://www.goodreads.com/quotes/5521-everything-you-can-imagine-is-real (accessed December 13, 2013).

1. Albert Einstein. See Goodreads website: http://www.goodreads.com/quotes/556030-imagination-is-more-important-than-knowledge-for-knowledge-is-limited (accessed December 13, 2013).
2. Neville Goddard, *The Power of Awareness* (Huey Global, 2012): p. 15.
3. Ascended Master Saint Germain, *The "I Am" Discourses*, Volume 19, Discourse 2 (Schaumburg, IL.: Saint Germain Press, 2011).
4. David Hawkins, *The Eye of the I* (kindle edition) (West Sedona, AZ.: Veritas Publishing, 2010).

Chapter 11   The Way to Learn: You Can Be a Step Ahead

Epigraph. Albert Einstein. See Goodreads website: http://www.goodreads.com/quotes/7090-the-intuitive-mind-is-a-sacred-gift-and-the-rational (accessed December 13, 2013).

1. James Twyman, *The Moses Code*, (Carlsbad, CA.: Hay House, 2008): p. 172.

Chapter 12   An Open Mind: Your Key to Beating Uncertainty

Epigraph. Dr. Seuss, *I Can Read with My Eyes Shut!* See Goodreads website: http://www.goodreads.com/quotes/234389-you-ll-miss-the-best-things-if-you-keep-your-eyes (accessed December 13, 2013).

1. Albert Einstein. See Goodreads website: http://www.goodreads.com/quotes/7275-in-the-middle-of-difficulty-lies-opportunity (accessed December 13, 2013).
2. Lao Tzu, *Tao Te Ching*, Jonathan Star, translator (New York: Penguin Group, 2008): p. 56.

Chapter 13   Patience: Your Thousand-Mile Journey

Epigraph. Lao Tzu, *Tao Te Ching*, Jonathan Star, translator (New York: Penguin Books, 2008): p. 83.

1. Ascended Master Saint Germain, *The "I Am" Discourses*, Volume 19, Discourse 4 (Schaumburg, IL.: Saint Germain Press, 2011).

Chapter 14   Meditation: Your Calm Revolution

Epigraph. Sri Nisargadatta Maharaj. See website: http://www.goodreads.com/quotes/117548-a-quiet-mind-is-all-you-need-all-else-will (accessed December 13, 2013).

Chapter 15   Synchronicity: Tapping into the Power of Your Highest Self

Epigraph. Carl Jung, *Memories, Dreams, Reflections* (New York: Random House, 1989): p. 401. Recorded and edited by Aniela Jaffe and translated by Richard and Clara Winston.